CW01468158

SOME NOTES ABOUT PST TOMOWO···

'Pastor Adetomowo Faduyile George. I have a rare opportunity to read through some of your books on Christian religious topics. I am amazed by the high level of research into the words of God as revealed in your well articulated, inspiring and redeeming books. At a stage, I became confused if the write-up could have emanated from a pharmacist with little or no bias to Christian religion. The topic and soul winning books authored by a Princess of a Prominent Traditional Ruler in whose palace, traditional, Christian and other religious practices compete, I hesitate not in recommending to all and sundry the books for reading and studying to witness how God works.'

- His Royal Majesty, Oba Alayeluwa George Babatunde Faduyile,
The Abodi of Ikaleland, Ondo State, Nigeria.

'Pastor tomowo is a trained consultant pharmacist who is fervent for the Lord. Her burning desire to reach people across geographical borders of nations through the Church in the Air has blessed many homes and individuals. May our Lord prosper her vision and continually renew her anointing'

- Dr Kayode Afolabi,
Consultant Obstetrician and Gynaecologist,
Director, Reproductive Health, Federal Ministry of Health, Abuja, Nigeria

'I am being blessed by the messages by Pst Tomowo. They are very relevant, inspiring, and encouraging. Thank you, Pst Tomowo for your care for the body to share this with us. God bless you'.

- Randi Corkey.
Almond, New York, USA

'I have known pastor tomowo for almost two years now. She loves God very dearly and she has a very good understanding of God's word that she teaches weekly. Focusing on contemporary topics and issues that are relevant to the needs of believers hungry for the truth of God's word and how to apply that truth in living out the Christian life victoriously in the 21st century''.

- Gabriel Okougha
Resident Pastor, KICC, The Fountain of Grace,
Gray, Essex, London, United Kingdom

'Pastor Tomowo, my very close friend and sister, is my most spiritual female friend grounded in the ways and acts of God. I know undoubtedly that she does not only have God but knows and walk with Him intimately –and unto this, she's sold out. She lives a life of wholeness both on and off the pulpit'.

- Dr Oyinbo Manuel,
Resident Pastor, Kingsway International Christian Centre,
Windhoek, Namibia.

'Pastor Tomowo is... A true lover of the Lord Jesus. Passionate about the kingdom of God. Committed to enlightening saints with the truth of Christ'.

- Pastor Bankie Olusina.
Kingdom –Word Ministries,
Enugu, Nigeria.

THE 3RD PERSON IN MARRIAGE SERIES. . .

THE PREPARATIONS

Focusing on the Foundation of Marriage!

The 3rd Person in Marriage

series...

THE PREPARATIONS

The Church in the A...

pst tomowo

Unless otherwise indicated, all Scripture quotations marked (NKJV) are from *the New King James Bible.* Copyright © 1979, 1980, 1982 by Thomas Nelson, Inc. Used by permission. All rights reserved. Scriptures quotations taken from the Amplified Bible (AMP), Copyright © 2015 by The Lockman Foundation Used by permission. www.Lockman.org. Scripture quotations marked (KJV) taken from the *King James Version of the Holy Bible.*

The 3rd Person in Marriage series... THE PREPARATIONS

[Maiden Edition]

©2020 pst tomowo

The Church in the Air.

ISBN: 9798574604731

The church in the Air publications.

1192 Rising Moon Trail,

Snellville, GA, 30078, USA

Website: www.air.church

Email: info@air.church

Library of Congress Control Number:

2020910095

All right reserved. No part of this book reproduced or transmitted in any form or by any means, electronic or mechanical – including photocopying, recording, or by any information storage and retrieval system ... without the prior written consent of the publisher. All enquires to be directed to info@air.church

Publisher's note:

The reader should not regard the recommendations, ideas and lifestyle practices expressed and described in this book as a substitute for the advice of certified medical specialists or other professionals and experts. The application of such expressed therein is at the reader's sole discretion and risk.

UNTO GOD . . .

'Out of the eater came forth meat, and out of the strong came forth sweetness' (Judges 14:14)

"For this reason shall a man leave his father and mother, and cleave to his wife, and they twain shall be one flesh: so then they are no longer twain, but one flesh. What therefore God hath joined together, let not man put asunder."

(Mark 10:7-9)

'And He said, Unto you it is given to know the mysteries of the kingdom of God: but to others in parables; that seeing they might not see, and hearing they might not understand.'

(Luke 8:10)

CONTENTS···

OVERVIEW…

THE 3RD PERSON IN MARRIAGE SERIES…

When the Spirit of GOD nudged me to take on this series, I was super reluctant… who will not, for this was where I failed the most in my life - Marriage… (I thought!)…

However, *'Out of the eater came forth meat, and out of the strong came forth sweetness' (Judges 14:14)* …

Right in the deepest valley of my failure…. I encountered the 3rd Person in Marriage, who began to reveal to me, step by step, precept upon precept, line upon line… how and why marriages fail… and why Marriage can be successful!

This revelation can only be Divine… *'For unto us it is given to know the mysteries of the Kingdom of GOD: but to others in parables'*… *(Luke 8:10)*

Spanning from the Understanding of Marriage to its Preparations, the Choosing, the Compatibilities, Multiplications and it's

Reigning...This book series will show you WHY your marriage is working, so you might keep at it ... or WHY it is not working, so you might see a customized way out for you. DISCLAIMER: STRICTLY FOR BELIEVERS!

The world today defines marriage in many ways including lusts, expressions of rebellion, lawlessness, diversities, anger, perversion, social status, even as a debased mindset... With us in the kingdom of CHRIST... It is different... Because we are GOD's people... And we carry GOD's presence...

There are millions of experts, mentors and coaches focusing on relationships, there are tons of books out there... Beyond all of these, because we are all involved in marriage, whether you are married or not, everyone is a product of a relationship between a man and a woman... Therefore, we all have a good degree of knowledge and information on how marriage works or how they are expected to be run for successful outcome...

We are therefore appealing to you... <u>have an open mind</u>... be receptive... maybe you can say a simple prayer... that GOD should help you see more... let this book series add to the knowledge you already have... and we pray that that will be the case in the Name of [1]YESHUA HAMASHIACH (JESUS CHRIST), Amen.

pst tomowo
... setting men up with GOD, for a GLORIOUS TURNAROUND!

---

[1] YESHUA HAMASHIACH is the original Hebrew Name translated to JESUS CHRIST

FAITH BOOST...

"Are you ready for this level… If we live in the Spirit… Let us also walk in the Spirit.

We live in the Spirit via waiting on GOD in Praise, Word and Spirit…

However, we walk in the Spirit when we are sensitive to the dictate of the Spirit in our daily dealings… Because GOD can cause a directive to come anytime and anywhere…

Violent faith makes you restful even in adversity… What you do not want… Do not watch. What you do not resist has the right to persist.

What you do not confront you cannot conquer… When GOD speaks… Everything and everyone hears…When the light comes from heaven… He puts you in command… You cannot pray off a prophetic agenda… you can only seek an exemption…

There is no safe place anywhere in the world… Except in CHRIST… Faith is to be received …brooded upon… when matured… released at the instance of the presence of the Anointing… then acted upon immediately afterwards." **(Excerpts from one of the messages of [2]Bishop David Oyedepo of Living Faith Church).**

………   ………   ………   ………

"Check your emotions at the door…Never think with your eyes… Because Satan will always show you something that you should see … to distract you. Believe with your hearts… Never you look at

the difficulty … It will cause you to disbelief the power within you… Above you and beneath you lies the power that is immeasurable and can change the whole world… Your part is not to create… You are to take advantage of what has already been created…

Ministry is a season of responsibility. Faith insists on possessing possessions… Faith will make you owe things… Faith insists on possessing… Faith refuses to let the heathen keep what belongs to you… Faith is not to be treated as an intellectual puzzle… It should be believed… You don't have to prove it…

Have conversations with GOD… He loves to talk… When you know GOD… Serving him will be easy… Faith never has to be proven… Faith is to be believed… Faith will work in your heart… even with doubt in your heart… If you can believe it.....That is all you are required of… All things are possible to him that believe… Spiritually… Physically… and Financially.

Emotional outburst can limit GOD… And cause you not to keep His word…Don't go by your soul… Follow your heart…Do not try to meet your own needs… Believe GOD… Do not believe for deficits… Go for 100 folds… 1000 times…" **(Excerpts from one of the messages of [3]Br. Jesse Duplantis. 'Check your emotions at the door')**

---

[3] Jesse Duplantis. www.jdm.org

SOME

FOUNDATIONAL

TRUTH ON

MARRIAGE

1. SOME FOUNDATIONAL TRUTH ON MARRIAGE ...

When the Spirit of GOD nudged me to take on this series, He told me that from the pages of the Bible lies in-depth insights and secrets to a successful relationship. When these revelations were been unfolded unto me... I was amazed, surprised at the depth of riches of GOD's knowledge...

'O the depth of the riches both of the wisdom and knowledge of God, how unsearchable are his judgements, and His ways past finding out.' (Romans 11:33, KJV)

Marriage originated from GOD hence fully understood through GOD...We are GOD's people... We are not of this world... Marriage is not what the world calls it... Lust, diversity, variation, expressions of perversion, anger and rebellion...

The originator has a Manual for Marriage. . . We will, therefore, be using His Manual: The Scripture, the very common stories of the Bible, to gain insights into the keys to a successful marriage.

Like everything created and valued by GOD, the enemy attacks Marriage immensely at every stage of its life cycle... − The

18

understanding stage, (wrong perspective and beliefs on marriage); preparatory stage, (wrong upbringing and abused childhood); choosing stage, (wrong timing and choice of partners, or lack of partner); fusion stage, (incompatibility at different levels); multiplication stage, (unfruitfulness physically, socially and spiritually); and reigning stage, (living in fulfilment in life)…

Today, as a result of these attacks, there are a lot of diversities and confusions about marriage, men with many wives, women with many husbands, multiple divorces, single parents, 'baby mamas', co-habiting partners, 'friends with benefits'… and all sorts of relationships, so much that one seems not to know what the ideal is any more today. .. As in the circular world so fully reflected in the churches and among the ministers of the Gospel…

Despite these confusions, let us trust the Holy Spirit open our eyes of understanding to gain insights into the 'IDEAL'; as expected; in the beginning; from the Marriage Manual… At least, for knowledge sake, knowing what is expected… and what is expected of us, believers! Irrespective of your degree of wholeness or brokenness, we pray that the Light of CHRIST shines on every dark and obscure area of your marriage and birth you a customized MIRACLE in JESUS name, Amen…

This book series aims at revealing the 'IDEAL', the standard with which one can easily stage one's relationship up with, thereby helping to see why we are succeeding in our relationships and keeping at it… as well as also seeing where one is falling short and what and what to do to make amends… Praying that as we dive into the revealed steps in marriage cycle, our eyes of understanding are opened to the gains and flaws in our relationships, to birth better relationships and marriage.

Because marriage involves different persons from mostly different backgrounds, the examples and practices in this book may require commitments, dedications and lifestyle modifications for its effectiveness. However, as with all the word of GOD, they forever settled in heaven and works if applied in faith under any conditions or circumstances. Let us dig into this . . .

UNDERSTANDING THE ELEMENTS OF MARRIAGE

In this chapter, we will be addressing the basic understanding of marriage... a little bit in-depth into the basic foundational truth in marriage. When this understanding is clear, then it becomes easier to see where each lack is and what to seek in pursuit of its amendment. Please as encouraged earlier, have an open mind to this and let the Spirit of GOD minister Life to you as you read on. We will be addressing Understanding of - In the beginning; The man in the marriage; The woman in the marriage; The third person in marriage; The Godly marriage; and Managing crisis at the understanding stage.

IN THE BEGINNING...

"In the beginning, GOD created the heavens and the earth. The earth was without form and void, and darkness was on the face of the deep. And the Spirit of God was hovering over the face of the waters. Then GOD said, "let there be light"; and there was light.

And GOD saw the light, that it was good; and God divided the light from the darkness." (Genesis 1:1-4 NKJV)

[15]"Therefore I also, after I heard of your faith in the Lord Jesus and your love for all the saints, [16]do not cease to give thanks for you, making mention of you in my prayers:

[17]The God of our Lord Jesus Christ, the father of glory, may give to you the Spirit of wisdom and revelation in the knowledge of him, [18]the eyes of your understanding being enlightened; that you may know what is the hope of his calling, what are the riches of the glory of his inheritance in the saints, [19]and what is the exceeding greatness of his power toward us who believe, according to the working of his mighty power" (Ephesians 1:15-19, NKJV)

[26]"then GOD said, "let us make man in our image, according to Our likeness; let them have dominion over the fish of the sea, over the birds of the air, and over the cattle, over all the earth and over every creeping thing that creeps on the earth." [27]So GOD created man in His own image; in the image of GOD he created him; male and female he created them. [28]Then God blessed them, and GOD said to them, "be fruitful and multiply; fill the earth and subdue it; have dominion over the fish of the sea, over the birds of the air, and over every living thing that moves on the earth." (Genesis 1:26-28, NKJV).

We are of CHRIST kingdom... We are of the light... We are of the day...

"In the beginning was the word, and the word was with GOD, and the word was GOD. [2]He was at the beginning with GOD. [3]All things

were made through him, and without him nothing was made that was made. ⁴In him was life, and the life was the light of men. ⁵And the light shines in the darkness, and the darkness did not comprehend it." (John 1:1-5, NKJV).

We are not of this world...

⁴"But you, brethren, are not in darkness, so that this day should overtake you as a thief. ⁵You are all sons of light and sons of the day. We are not of the night nor of darkness. ⁶Therefore let us not sleep, as others do, but let us watch and be sober." (1 Thessalonians 5:4-6, NKJV).

We thank GOD ... For unto us it is given to know and understand the mystery of CHRIST's kingdom...

'And He said, <u>Unto you it is given to know the mysteries of the kingdom of God</u>: but to others in parables; that seeing they might not see, and hearing they might not understand.' (Luke 8:10, KJV).

We are sanctified by the word... The light that shines forth over the darkness...

¹⁵"I do not pray that you should take them out of the world, but that you should keep them from the evil one. ¹⁶They are not of the world, just as I am not of the world. ¹⁷<u>Sanctify them by your truth.</u> Your word is truth." (John 17:15-17, NKJV).

There is 'HOW' it is been done in the kingdom of CHRIST... There is marriage according to the law of the kingdom of CHRIST... Irrespective of what the society accepts as 'correct' or 'the church' agreed as allowed. It is, however, a CHOICE to choose the way of the Kingdom of CHRIST! We pray for illumination in JESUS name, Amen

12"Giving thanks to the father who has qualified us to be partakers of the inheritance of the saints in the light. 13He has delivered us from the power of darkness and conveyed us into the kingdom of the son of his love, 14in whom we have redemption through his blood, the forgiveness of sins." (Colossians 1:12-14, NKJV).

GOD CREATED ADAM AS MALE AND FEMALE...

In the beginning, Adam was created as Male and Female. Complete. Lacking in nothing...

26And God said, Let us make man in our image, after our likeness: and let them have dominion over the fish of the sea, and over the fowl of the air, and over the cattle, and over all the earth, and over every creeping thing that creepeth upon the earth.

> **In the beginning, Adam was created as Male and Female. Complete. Lacking in nothing…**

27So God created man in his own image, in the image of God created He him; male and female created He them.

28And God blessed them, and God said unto them, Be fruitful, and multiply, and replenish the earth, and subdue it: and have dominion over the fish of the sea, and over the fowl of the air, and over every living thing that moveth upon the earth.' (Genesis 1:26-28, KJV)

This revelation is further confirmed in chapter five:

"This is the book of the generations of Adam._In the day that GOD created man, in the likeness of God made he him; <u>male and female created he them; and blessed them, and called their name Adam</u>, in the day when they were created." (Genesis 5:1-2 KJV)

[2]'And GOD <u>blessed them, and called their name Adam</u>'. Adam was created as male and female…. GOD created Adam complete, as a male and female. Wanting nothing!

Think about this.

Your Notes . . .

Take a second look at the above scriptures... write out your thoughts...

MAN AND WOMAN ARE DIFFERENT...

After the creation of Adam, GOD put him into the garden he had created for his pleasure and charged him to till and tend the garden. In the course of his duty, while taking care and charge of all the creatures GOD created, behold, none of the creatures of GOD was like Adam, hence Adam became lonely... Lonely not because He was not complete, he was lonely because there was no other creature exactly like... and GOD decided to make a companion for Adam.

> **Why Woman then?**
>
> **For a variety of man...So there is not only one type of Man...**

Why Woman then? For a variety of man...So there is not only one type of man...

How was the man was created... with a higher matter than the earth... The breath of GOD... So the man can have dominion over the earth. This is the mandate of dominion... The BLESSING.

[7]"*And the Lord God formed man of the dust of the ground, and* _breathed into his nostrils the breath of life_; *man became a living being.* [8]*The Lord God planted a garden eastward in Eden, _and there he put the man whom he had formed_." (Genesis 2:7-8 NKJV).*

The Lord perceived that Adam is the only creature in his class... the image of GOD... therefore the Lord promised to make a helpmeet for him... To make this need glaring... The Lord brought of all other creatures he created to Adam to see what he would call them...

Adam named all creature… and discovered none could meet as a companion for him…

"Then the Lord God took the man and put him in the garden of Eden to tend and keep it.' (Genesis 2:15, NKJV).

Because Adam was created completely ab-initio. Hence, it is simply logical that GOD separates the female part of Adam from him to make Eve!

And the Lord GOD said, *"it is not good that man should be alone; I will make him a helper comparable to him." (Genesis 2:16, NKJV)*

"So Adam gave names to all cattle, to the birds of the air, and to every beast of the field. But for Adam, there was not found a helper comparable to him.' (Genesis 2:20 NKJV).

Now, the gap is clear… Adam needs a companion. GOD needs to create another like Adam… Interestingly, the creator of the whole universe did not go the route of creating a separate being for Adam… He took from Adam to make his companion… why… Because Adam was created completely ab-initio. Hence, it is simply logical that He separates the female part of Adam from him to make Eve.

21'And the Lord God caused a deep sleep to fall on Adam, and he slept, and he took one of his ribs and closed up the flesh in its place. 22Then the rib which the Lord God had taken from man he made into a woman, and he brought her to the man." (Genesis 2:20-22, NKJV).

Point worth nothing...

GOD removed Eve from Adam. Therefore, at the appearance of Eve, Adam becomes incomplete, Eve becomes incomplete.

Therefore, Eve is the completion of Adam. This is why... if the woman is the completion of the Man, Then Man and woman are different!

> *GOD removed Eve from Adam. Therefore, at the appearance of Eve, Adam becomes incomplete, Eve becomes incomplete.*
>
> *Man and Woman are different...*

The woman is the completion of the Man. . . .

Adam... is different from Eve. They can never be the same. They will never be the same... They are different. Hence a need for a unifying force in relationships ... Like a glue to fix the puzzle into shape...

The woman is the complete part of Man, therefore, without a Man, the woman is incomplete... and without a woman, man is incomplete!

Pause, ponder and think about this ...

Your Notes . . .

A man is different from a woman... can you spot these differences around you...

THE 3RD PERSON IN MARRIAGE...

Adam will never be complete without Eve... And vice versa... If this is the case... then there is a need for a unifying force that will always join both!

The all-wisdom GOD decided to fuse Himself into the equation... after all, Adam (as Male and Female) was created in His image and likeness... Now that there is a separation, the GOD factor also is to be brought to fore...

> *Adam will never be complete without Eve... And vice versa... If this is the case... then there is a need for a unifying force that will always join both!*

Adam was in the habit of naming all creatures that GOD brought to him, and whatsoever he called them, became their names. After a forced sleep, Eve was presented unto Adam as usual, however, Adam saw for the first time, a different kind of creature. 'Bone of my bone'.

Moreover, while Adam was being presented his new companion, which was originally part of him, Adam saw beyond the woman, Adam also saw the Spirit of Marriage that joined them together!

For this reason... A man shall leave his father and mother and cleaved to his wife ... And they shall become one... he said.

[23] *"And Adam said: "This is now <u>bone of my bones</u> and flesh of my flesh; <u>she shall be called woman because she was taken out of</u>*

man." ²⁴Therefore a man shall leave his father and mother and be joined to his wife, <u>and they shall become one flesh.</u> ²⁵And they were both naked, the man and his wife, and were not ashamed." *(Genesis 2:23-25 NKJV).*

How did Adam understand these two mysteries… Well at that time, Adam was still operating at his highest frequency … at the order of God, hence understood the deep things of GOD.

Adam knew by intuition that Eve was taken out of him, hence called her woman. He equally knew that there must be a cleaving of man and woman for them to become One Flesh...

GOD is the 3rd Person in Marriage.

The Cleaving Force…

The central force of unity...

GOD is the third person in marriage. The Cleaving Force… The central force of unity...

This truth, further revealed across the scriptures as follows…

A Prophet, Malachi, revealed the mind of GOD concerning this truth:

¹⁴"You ask, "Why?" It is because <u>the Lord is the witness between you and the wife of your youth.</u> You have been unfaithful to her, though she is your partner, the wife of your marriage covenant. ¹⁵Has not the <u>One God made you?</u> You belong to him in body and Spirit. <u>And what does the One GOD seek?</u> Godly offspring. So be on your guard, and do not be unfaithful to the wife of your youth." *(Malachi 2:14-15, NIV)*

[14]*"Yet ye say, Wherefore? Because the Lord hath been witness between thee and the wife of thy youth, against whom thou hath dealt treacherously: yet is she thy companion, and the wife of thy covenant.* [15]*And did not He make One? Yet had He the residue of the Spirit. And wherefore one? That he might seek a Godly seed. Therefore take heed to your Spirit, and let none deal treacherously against the wife of his youth."* (Malachi 2:15, KJV)

[14]*'Yet you ask, Why does He reject it? Because the Lord was witness [to the covenant made at your marriage] between you and the wife of your youth, against whom you have dealt treacherously and to whom you were faithless. Yet she is your companion and the wife of your covenant [made by your marriage vows]. [15]And did not God make [you and your wife] one [flesh]? Did not One make you and preserve your spirit alive? And why [did God make you two] one? Because He sought a godly offspring [from your union]. Therefore take heed to yourselves, and let no one deal treacherously and be faithful to the wife of his youth.'* (Malachi 2:14-15, AMP).

> **GOD is the Spirit of Marriage...**
>
> **The ONE that makes the couple one!**

[14]*'Do you know why? Simple. Because GOD was there as a witness when you spoke your marriage vows to your young bride, and now you've broken these vows, broken the faith-bond with your vowed companion, your covenant wife. [15]GOD, not you, made marriage. His Spirit inhabits even the smallest details of marriage. And what*

does He want from marriage? Children of God, that's what. So guard the Spirit of marriage within you. Don't cheat on your spouse'. (Malachi 2:14-15, MSG).

GOD is the Spirit of Marriage... The ONE that makes the couple one!

ONE God, The ONE... The SPIRIT... all these addressing the 3rd Person in Marriage!

Our Lord JESUS CHRIST made it clear...

It is GOD that joins Man and Woman in a union!

Our Lord JESUS CHRIST also brought this Truth out so clearly in two instances when asked questions relating to marriage. He made it clear that it is GOD that joins Man and Woman. He is the 3rd Person in Marriage...

[4]"And He answered and said to them, 'Have you not read that He who made them at the beginning made them male and female, [5] and said, 'For this reason a man shall leave his father and mother and be joined to this wife, and the two shall become one flesh'? [6]So then, they are no longer two but one flesh. Therefore what God has joined together, let not man separate." (Matthew 19:4-6, NKJV).

On another occasion, He pointed this Truth out again...

[5]"And Jesus answered and said to them, 'Because of the hardness of your heart he (Moses) wrote you this precept. [6]But from the beginning of the creation, God 'made them male and female.' [7]For

this reason a man shall leave his father and mother and be joined to his wife, [8]and the two shall become one flesh'; so then they are no longer two, but one flesh, [9]<u>therefore what GOD has joined together, let not man separate.</u>" (Mark 10:9, NKJV).

Our Lord JESUS CHRIST made it clear... It is GOD that joins Man and Woman in a union! Hence, admonishing men not to put this asunder because of the free will choice given them.

Finally still on this Truth, the Spirit of GOD furthermore revealed this through Apostle Paul as follows:

[14]*'For this cause I bow my knees unto the Father of our Lord Jesus Christ, [15]<u>Of whom the whole family in heaven and earth is named.</u>' (Ephesians 3:14-15, KJV).*

The whole family in heaven and earth named of GOD... Hello somebody... The 3rd Person in Marriage.

The father of our Lord JESUS CHRIST ... Of whom the whole family in heaven and on earth is named... The residue of GOD in all marriage... The oneness of GOD in marriage... The Spirit of marriage...

"For this reason I bow my knees to the father of our Lord JESUS CHRIST, from whom the whole family in heaven and earth is named," (Ephesians 3:14-15, NKJV).

AMEN... AMEN... AMEN...

Acknowledging and referencing this Spirit... in marriage ... Is key to your success in it...

Of whom the whole family in heaven and on earth is named... Is your family named of GOD? Have you received your already named family in GOD... When you submit to the one that named your family... You receive grace to love your wife... And grace to be submissive to your husband...

> *Marriage is between GOD, a Man and a Woman.*
>
> *Man and Woman are different, hence The Spirit of Marriage present to join them.*

Adam spoke of Him when Eve was brought to him... Prophet Malachi revealed Him as the ONE that makes them one... The Spirit of Marriage... Our Lord JESUS CHRIST made it clear once and for all... 'What GOD has joined together,..' and Apostle Paul revealed Him as the One of whom the whole family in heaven and earth is named!

The 3rd Person in Marriage...

Marriage is between GOD, a Man and a Woman. Man and Woman are different, hence The Spirit of Marriage present to join them.

If your eyes of understanding can grasp this, you are made forever.

Without the 3rd Person in Marriage, there can never be a genuine fusion in Marriage. The 3rd Person in Marriage JOINS the two separate and different beings... fuses them to become one flesh.

Therefore, every marriage is a MIRACLE!

Man and Woman are different; they can never be the same nor be connected and compatible without the help of the 3rd Person in Marriage... The Spirit of Marriage... The ONE that makes them one!

Therefore, every marriage is a MIRACLE!

Your every marriage is a MIRACLE! The 3rd Person in Marriage makes the union worth it... It will take your conscious will of choice to put this asunder!

Pause, ponder and think about this ...

Your Notes . . .

What GOD has joined together... let no man put asunder... Is your marriage up to you ... or up to GOD...

The 3rd Person in Marriage

THE CHARACTERISTICS OF THE 1ST MAN

2. THE CHARACTERISTICS OF THE 1st MAN···

THE CHARACTERISTICS OF THE 1ST MAN

*F*rom the scriptures also revealed the basic characteristics of the man in the first marriage. Let us see the basic traits that Adam possessed at the first marriage ever... This will help reveal the mind of GOD on who is the man in marriage. The three basic elements of the man in marriage are as follows:

1. DOMINION AND AUTHORITY...

Dominion and Authority... wanting to take charge, wanting to be in control is one of the foremost characteristics of a man. Have you wonder where the phrase 'Man ego' comes from...

Although many lost this trait in upbringing, however, because it is key to manhood, men fight for this even in face of nothingness.

Dominion and Authority is the very first quality GOD endowed Adam. When GOD created Adam, He gave him the mandate of Fruitfulness.

'And God blessed them, and God said unto them, Be fruitful, and multiply, and replenish the earth, and subdue it: and have dominion over the fish of the sea, and over the fowl of the air, and over every living thing that moveth upon the earth.' (Genesis 1:28 KJV)

Then, GOD placed him in the garden to tend and care for it. GOD gave Adam dominion mandate… GOD brought to Adam all the creatures He created to name them, and whatsoever Adam called them remains their name. Dominion mandate.

Wonder why in Marriage, the name of the Man is very important. Here it is. Man's dominion and authority are expressed with their domain and territory acquisition. Man wants to dominate, acquire, and build a castle and kingdom for himself. This is how they are been wired. Once they acquire someone or something, they are looking for other things to acquire … You hear them say often… 'my wife'… 'my house'… 'my car'… my family'…

my… my… my… Dominion and Authority!

[15]'And the Lord God took the man, and put him into the garden of Eden to dress and to keep it. [19]And out of the ground the Lord God formed every beast of the field, and every fowl of the air, and brought them unto Adam to see what he would call them: and whatsoever Adam called every living creature, that was the name thereof.' (Genesis 2:15,19, KJV).

For Adam to have dominion, GOD submitted all other creatures into his hands. Adam named them… hence having dominion over them. He named Eve also… Could it be why woman and children take after the names of their father?

> **For Adam to have dominion, GOD submitted all other creatures into his hands.**
>
> **Adam named them… hence having dominion over them.**
>
> **He named Eve also…**

[6]*'But one in a certain place testified, saying, What is man, that thou art mindful of him? Or the son of man, that thou visitest him?* [7]*Thou madest him a little lower than the angels, thou crownest him with glory and honour, and didst set him over the works of thy hands.* [8]*Thou hast put all things in subjection under his feet.* For in that He put all in subjection under him, he left nothing that is not put under him. But now we see not yet all things put under him.'* (Hebrews 2:6-8, KJV).

Dominion and Authority is the very first characteristic of the Man. Having a sphere and domain to dominate, and authority to take charge over… When men are denied this trait, it is as if, they are stripped naked. Take a second look at the men in your life… and you will smell dominion, authority from a distance…

2. VISION AND DIRECTION…

Secondly, Man is the one with Vision and Direction… Dominion and Authority work hand in hand with Vision and Direction. The singularity of Purpose. Understanding the path to take.

GOD gave Adam instructions on what to do and what not to do in the garden… GOD gave Adam the vision and Direction for life. This is the reason why man is unilateral in thinking… Focus!

> *GOD gave Adam instructions on what to do and what not to do in the garden…*
>
> *GOD gave Adam the Vision and Direction for life.*
>
> *The reason why man is unilateral in thinking… Focus!*

Man is the one with the vision, direction… Man has foresight… It is expected that man take the lead in Vision and direction for the union.

[17]'And the Lord God took the man, and put him into the garden of Eden to dress it and to keep it. [18]And the Lord God commanded the man, saying, Of every tree of the garden thou mayest freely eat. [19]But of the tree of the knowledge of good and evil, thou shall not eat of it: for in the day that thou eatest thereof thou shall surely die.' (Genesis 2:17-19, KJV).

Adam was the one with the clear-cut instructions, (Vision and Direction) for their lives. This task was not repeated with Eve. Because it was expected, that Adam relayed the Vision and

Direction to his wife. I guess he failed at this and this lacuna spoke for itself!

Vision birth singularity of Purpose. This is why man focuses mainly on one thing at a time. 'I want to eat'… however, after food, he moves on to another thing, and forgets about food immediately…

This trouble women a great deal… 'I want sex'… and while the woman is still brooding afterwards over the pleasure, men are up and off they go… why????… Vision and Direction… Focusing on a Goal per time.

> *No matter how good or bad the stuff may be, once men have acquired it, they are done.*
>
> *'What is the next thing on agenda'… they will say…*

This is the reason boredom is a major weakness or issue with men. No matter how good or bad the stuff may be, once men have acquired it, they are done. 'What is the next thing on agenda'… they will say… Repeating the same things over and can be seen as boredom or nagging to them…

Understanding this trait will help a great deal in dealing with this unique species of GOD… Man!

3. STABILITY…

The third basic characteristic of the Man is Stability. Physical strength … Roughness…Toughness… No hormonal changes … No monthly cycle...Stability... Men are just there. Stable... Ever ready...

Why this Stability, to sustain the weaker vessel made not as stable...Men are wired to be stable... Not for selfish display, it is to sustain every other thing that is not as stable...

This characteristic is obvious in men today... As a woman, I wonder many times why men are so rough, big, strong, and with no hormonal mood swing... This is because they are to bring Stability to the union.

To make a woman from the first man, only one rib from his side was removed! There is no way the human being made from one rib could be as strong and stable as the former!... On presenting the new human to Adam, He knew she was <u>a bone of his bones</u>, and flesh of his flesh.... And he named her woman... This is Stability...

[21]*"And the Lord God caused a deep sleep to fall upon Adam, and he slept: <u>and He took one of his ribs, and closed up the flesh instead thereof;</u>* [22]*And the rib, which the Lord God had taken from man, made he a woman, and brought her unto the man.* [23]*and Adam said: "This is now <u>bone of my bones</u> and flesh of my flesh; <u>she shall be called woman because she was taken out of man.</u>" (Genesis 2:21-23, NKJV).*

It is a wrong assumption to think or believe that men and women are equal and the same... irrespective of civilization, education and socialization exposure... men and women are different...

45

however, men and women deserve an equal right to health, education, wealth, and all the good of life.

Today, this Stability is used as a tool to oppress women in many settings... the same trait that was meant to protect is used to abuse women... these things ought not to be so.

Why this Stability, to sustain the weaker vessel made not as stable...

Men are wired to be stable... Not for selfish display, it is to sustain every other thing that is not as stable...

There may be more characteristics of the man, however, these three traits form the bedrock on which every other traits and quality are built upon. Such as Financial strength fuelling Dominion and Authority, Education and /or Skill expertise boosting the Vision and Direction of the Union, and the Stability... (Fill in others you know ...)

Dominion and Authority... Vision and Direction ... Stability... what a BLESSING to see these expressed in the world today!

Your Notes:

What are the characteristics of the man you (or your man) possess...

The 3rd Person in
Person in
Marriage

THE
CHARACTERISTICS
OF THE 1ST
WOMAN

3. CHARACTERISTICS OF THE 1ˢᵀ WOMAN ⋯

THE CHARACTERISTICS OF THE WOMAN

*A*s with the Man, GOD did not leave the woman empty. GOD endowed the woman with her traits. The first woman, Eve possessed these traits ...

This is fully expressed in Genesis chapters two and three. As Eve expressed herself in Genesis chapter 3, her traits and qualities were revealed... What are these qualities...

1. SMARTNESS AND INTUITION ...

Smartness is the very first quality of the first woman in Marriage. Remember GOD says she is a HELP MEET... that means a Solution Hub... This Smartness can also be called Instinct, or Intuition.

"and the Lord GOD said, it is not good that the man should be alone; I will make <u>him an help meet for him</u>.' (Genesis 2:18, NKJV).

A HELPMEET, A Solution Hub can be liking to today's search engine such as Google... Once you type in something into the Solution Hub... it or she browses around and give you all possible outcomes to the request.

> *A HELPMEET, A Solution Hub can be liking to today's search engine such as Google...*
>
> *Once you type in something into the Solution Hub... it or she browses around and give you all possible outcomes to the request.*

This is the very first trait of the woman. SMARTNESS... A HELP MEET... A SOLUTION HUB... think about this...

Have you wondered where in the world women get their wisdom from? Men and women will be exposed to the same thing, and the woman will see deeper things about the stuff... Smartness... So much that this has landed many women into been bullied, abused, and oppressed... ''Why does she know so much... let us stop her!''

To buttress this point, Let us look at how Eve acted by the forbidden Tree... The Bible says both Eve and Adam were standing by the Tree. This was the main mistake... Remember GOD gave Adam the Vision and Direction... 'Dress and keep the Garden'... however, Adam was not at his duty post.

Unfortunately, Eve, a solution hub, a HELP MEET will always proffer help and solution everywhere and anywhere she is found.

51

And since they were both standing by the forbidden tree... Eve went to work. And the enemy took advantage of her smartness to beguile her...

Let us see the rendition below:

'Now the serpent was more subtle than any beast of the field which the Lord God had made. And he said to the woman, Yea, hath God said, Ye shall not eat of every tree of the garden?

²And the woman said unto the serpent, We may eat of the fruit of the trees of the garden: ³But of the fruit of the tree which is in the midst of the garden, God hath said, Ye shall not eat of it, neither shall ye touch it, lest ye die. ⁴And the serpent said unto the woman, Ye shall not surely die: ⁵For God doth know that in the day ye ate thereof, then your eyes shall be opened, and ye shall be as gods, knowing good and evil.

⁶And when the woman saw that the tree was good for food, and that it was pleasant to the eyes, and a tree to be desired to make one wise, she took of the fruit thereof, and did eat, and gave also to her husband with her, and he did eat.' (Genesis 3:1-6, KJV).

Adam and Eve were by the tree... Not on the vision, tilling the garden. ... Eve as a helpmeet will always bring a solution to anywhere and anything she is exposed to... hence, she browsed the tree... And saw three reasons why she must eat of it...

⁶'And when the woman saw that the tree was good for food, and that it was pleasant to the eyes, and a tree to be desired to make one wise, she took of the fruit thereof,..' (Genesis 3:6)

The Devil through serpent did not tell her those… she saw them by herself. She browsed the tree deeply… and saw many reasons why to eat of it… versus the only one reason GOD gave Adam!

Instinct… Smartness… Insight into things… Multi-dimensional. She brought help to the wrong place. Do you see this in women today… Eve was not properly informed of the Vision; secondly, Adam was not at his duty post, hence exposing all of the smartness of Eve to the wrong thing and wrong place!

> **Adam and Eve were by the tree... Not on the vision, tilling the garden. ...**
>
> **Eve as a helpmeet will always bring a solution to anywhere and anything she is exposed to…**
>
> **she browsed the tree... And saw three reasons why she must eat of it...**

Smartness… Intuition… Instinct… No man can compete with the smartness and instinct of a woman. GOD made them the Solution Hub. Hence had abilities to reason at multi-dimensional level…

The enemy told Eve of one reason to eat the fruit… Eve saw three reasons why she could not miss eating the fruit. Smartness… Instinct… The intuition of a woman is unparalleled. Any man that tries to compete with a woman does that at his peril.

Today, many men stoop so low to get a very small, young and

Uneducated girls to marry … and to their surprise, in a few years, those unexposed girls are in control… Smartness, Intuition of a woman. My advice, do not compete with a woman!… (Just a joke)

2. INFLUENCE…

The very second trait of a woman as seen in the life of the first woman, Eve is INFLUENCE… Though women are not endowed to lead, dominate or have directions… However, the woman is highly equipped for Influence. Women influence Authority… Women influence Leaders, Women influence Dominion… Women influence Visions… Women influence Strongmen… Think about this.

"And when the woman saw that the tree was good for food, and that it was pleasant to the eyes, and a tree to be desired to make one wise, <u>she took of the fruit thereof, and did eat, and gave also unto her husband with her; and he did eat</u>." (Genesis 3:6, KJV)

Eve did not only eat the fruit, she gave the fruit also to her husband with her… and he ate!

"Behold, thy people in the midst of thee are women: the gates of thy land shall be set wide open unto thine enemies: the fire shall devour thy bars." (Nahum 3:13 KJV)

Although natural women are not given Vision and Direction, nor can they lead effectively… however, what is home with women is the ability to influence Authority. Because of her multi-dimensional approach to things, a woman will see all the possible way to influence Authority.

This is why the enemy did not bother to attack Adam directly. Or else, Adam, a unilaterally focused being, will simply reply the serpent that GOD says we should not eat of it'...

However, with Eve, one reason is not enough to convince her, she saw three good reasons to eat of the fruit, she took it and ate, afterwards, prevailed over her husband, who simply obey instructions. Oh, we are to eat now, okay... while GOD's instruction was standing, Adam stuck to it, now a new instruction is here from Eve, 'Eat... and he said, yes ma!

Delilah asked Samson of the secret to his power, three times, she used it against him the three times, yet Samson kept revealing it to her... until she brought doom to him!

> *The Influential ability of the woman is because of her multi-dimensional way of reasoning...*
>
> *A woman will see things in so many ways, and try all the many ways until she gets her way!*

The Influential ability of the woman is because of her multi-dimensional way of reasoning... woman will see things in so many ways, and try all the many ways until she gets her way!

This is why women talk a lot... as their brain is working multi-dimensionally, they slip off through the mouth in many ways too... [4]Science had confirmed that the part of the brain that controls speech also control most

---

[4] What part of the brain controls speech?, www.healthline.com

of the body... Therefore, talkativeness is home with women... because their brain works even in silence... When and if a woman set out to acquire something... she may get it, eventually...

The influence of a woman is unparalleled. A solution hub. Saddled with several ways to achieve things... one out of her million ways will hit the target!

Hmmmmmmmmm....

3. BEAUTY . . .

The last but not the least is BEAUTY... Beauty is a characteristic of the first woman. Adam was captivated by his woman... Having seen and named several creatures... when Adam saw Eve... He went all the way for her. She is 'the bone of my bones, flesh of my flesh'...

Have you wondered why women are so pretty, shapely, soft – talking, sweet voice, soft face, cool smile, waist twisting, slim arms, ... think about that... BEAUTY... this is a trait endowed every woman.

[22]And the rib, which the Lord God had taken from man, made he a woman, and brought her unto the man. [23]and Adam said: "This is now bone of my bones and flesh of my flesh; she shall be called woman because she was taken out of man." (Genesis 2:22-23, NKJV).

Forever, man will always have eyes for the beauty of the woman. It is evident in our world today. So much that, women's beauty is been used as a tool for all manner of evil deeds. Such as advertisement, influence, to set trap for great men... etc.

Abraham, understanding this, traded his wife for his security...

"and it came to pass, when he was come near to enter into Egypt, that he said unto Sarai his wife, Behold now, I know that thou art a fair woman to look upon:" (Genesis 12:11 KJV)

"And in all the land were no women found so fair as the daughters of Job: and their father gave them inheritance among their brethren." (Job 42:15, KJV)

Forever, man will always have eyes for the beauty of the woman.

This is evident in our world today.

These three characteristics of the woman: Smartness, Influence and Beauty were not made in an error by GOD. The woman was made with good intention. However, the offence of the woman caused so much havoc to creation that if this not addressed, one might not come to appreciate the actual purpose of the traits of the woman. I have heard from many quarters that women are the source of trouble in the world... Hmmmmmm...

Let us take a look into this...

THE OFFENSE OF THE WOMAN . . .

The multi-dimensional ways of seeing things and reasoning drives woman not to be able to stick to one direction or authority… This may come up as no reference nor regards to vision and direction because it is not in her… Hence must always be under the guidance…

Women naturally present as lawbreakers… they simply enjoy breaking the rules, their makeup gives them multiple options and when not guided, they will explore these options even at the expense of breaking GOD's law and instructions. This was what happened in the Garden of Eden. Eve could not adhere to a single law without Adam's supporting and insisting Vision and Direction.

> *This is the Offense of the Woman.*
>
> *Applying the Smartness, Intuition, Influence and her Beauty on wrong things and in wrong places…*

This is the Offense of the Woman. Applying the Smartness, Intuition and Influence on wrong things and in wrong places…

This has led many women to usurp authority instead of influencing it… As a helpmeet, a solution hub, care must be taken to guide a natural woman in the right direction, or else, she will become a solution for evil deeds!

This is why, a woman that has no external support of vision and direction, may derail so badly, leading to pains and destructions.

According to the scriptures: the single lady must be under her father and a married lady under her husband's guidance... She can be easily deceived when not guided...'Satan tempted and deceived Eve... Not Adam' says the scriptures.

However, Eve influenced Adam... This still happens today... Delilah and Samson... She pressed on him several times..., yet, Samson fell all the time!

Because of the nature of the woman, a multi-dimensional rationing being, if she is not helped and support with vision and directions, (a trait she does not possess naturally), she can be gullible to distractions and instability. Let us see what the Spirit of GOD told Moses to do for the Israelites in this wise:

5"But if her father disallows her in the day that he heareth; not any of her vows, or of her bonds wherewith she hath bound her soul, shall stand: and the Lord shall forgive her, because her father disallowed her. 6And if she had at all an husband, when she vowed, or uttered ought out of her lips, wherewith she bound her soul; 7and her husband heard it, and held his peace at her in the day that he heard it: then her vows shall stand, and her bonds wherewith she bound her soul shall stand. 8But if her husband disallowed her on the day that he heard it; then he shall make her vow which she vowed, and that which she uttered with her lips, wherewith she bound her soul, of none effect: and the Lord shall forgive her." (Numbers 30:5-8, KJV)

Women according to the custom of Israelites were to be in guidance of a sort, always.

In today's world, promoting women freedom from oppression, (which is okay, by the way), ... sometimes goes into the extreme, where women become unaccountable to anyone, ... Now, this is a dangerous state to be in, if there is no external guiding support of some sort for her.

An ungodly woman is the most dangerous tool a man can have...Satan knows this... And he uses women greatly for evil deeds today. A free-spirited woman is a dangerous tool in the hands of the evil ones.

"As a Jewel of gold in a swine's snout, so is a fair woman which is without discretion." (Proverbs 11:22, KJV)

Moreover, as the brain of a woman function multi-dimensionally, so also is her mouth...hence, talkativeness is a very common weakness of a woman. No wonder the scriptures enjoin women to be in silence in church... (Not the Spirit-controlled women, of course!)

GOD suffers not a woman to preach... A natural woman... A non-Spirit-controlled woman cannot handle the things of GOD right! They are rather to learn in silence...

"Let a woman learn in silence with all submission." (1 Timothy 2:11, NKJV)

"And I do not permit a woman to teach or to have authority over a man, but to be in silence." (1 Timothy 2:12, NKJV)

"But I suffer not a woman to teach, nor to usurp authority over the man, but to be in silence." (1 Timothy 2:12, KJV)

Good news…there is a way out of this offence of the woman… let us get to it.

THE WOMAN AT REDEMPTION…

"But one of the soldiers pierced his side with a spear, and immediately blood and water came out." (John 19:34, NKJV)

JESUS CHRIST was pierced at his side…The same spot from where the rib that was made into a woman was removed… For the redemption of this great offence…

I was in a conference one day in London, UK; among ministers in a lobby during the break, and was sharing the thoughts on the 3rd Person in Marriage with a dear minister from Seychelles… She fixed her eyes on the picture of JESUS CHRIST handing on the wall and spoke this forth:

'JESUS CHRIST was pierced at his side… the exact same spot woman was removed from…''.

I was awed… wa oooo… remember, Matthew 18:20… *'For where two or three are gathered together in my Name, there am I in the midst of them'*. The Spirit of GOD gave her that insight… wa oooo… (I promised that I would always reference her whenever I share on this point! Her name is [5]Pst Maria Payet, wife of a pastor of one of the Redeemed Church of God, Seychelles). As a minister, countless

---

[5] Pastor Maria Payet, of Redeemed Church of God, Seychelles

revelations had been granted me in the gatherings of the saints! Our GOD is GOOD and His Mercies endure forevermore, Amen.

Pause, Ponder, and think about this!

At redemption, this offence was done with. And all the curses that go with this offence had been redeemed by the Blood of our Lord Jesus Christ.

The Bibles says we are redeemed by the Blood of our Lord JESUS CHRIST… including the sins of the offence of the first woman.

'In whom we have redemption through His Blood, even the forgiveness of sins.' (Colossians 1:14, NKJV).

Therefore, as many as are led by the Spirit of GOD… These are the sons of GOD… For in CHRIST… No male, no female, no Jew, no gentile, no bond, no free…

"There is therefore now no condemnation to them which are in CHRIST JESUS, who walk not after the flesh, but after the Spirit." (Romans 8:1, KJV)

When a natural woman receives our Lord JESUS CHRIST as her Lord and Saviour, and submit to the Lordship of the Holy Spirit, She becomes guided, and influenced by the Holy Spirit that now lives inside of her… hence submitting to other authorities becomes easy.

²⁸"There is neither Jew nor Greek, there is neither bond nor free, there is neither male nor female: for ye are all one in CHRIST JESUS.

[29]*And if you are Christ's, then you are Abraham's seed, and heirs according to the promise." (Galatians 3:28-29, KJV)*

[10]*"And have put on the new man, which is renewed in knowledge after the image of him that created him:* [11]*where there is neither Greek nor Jew, circumcision nor uncircumcision, barbarian, Scythian, bond nor free: but CHRIST is all, and in all." (Colossians 3:10-11, KJV)*

> **A Godly woman is the most precious tool that any man can possess …**
>
> **He that finds a wife, finds a good thing...And obtained favour from the Lord...**

"For as many as are led by the Spirit of God, they are the sons of GOD." (Romans 8:14, KJV)

A Godly woman is the most precious tool that any man can possess ...He that finds a wife, finds a good thing...And obtained favour from the Lord...

This is why the scriptures enjoin wives to submit to her husband. For this is good and help to make good use of her Smartness, Instinct, intuition, influence and beauty.

"Wives, submit yourselves unto your own husbands, as it is fit in the Lord. Husbands, love your wives, and be not bitter against them." (Colossians 3:18-19, KJV)

"Wives, submit yourselves unto your own husbands, as unto the Lord." (Ephesians 5:22 KJV).

As a redeemed woman, led and ruled by the Holy Ghost, submitting to the husband or those in authority will never be an issue.

WOMAN IN SILENCE...

One day I asked the Spirit of GOD about the above scriptures on 'Women be silent in church'... and I heard: 'What do one do actively in silence'? ... I thought for some moments and this came out: Prayers...Prayers...Prayers...Prayers...

With the activeness and multi-dimensional nature of woman, keeping silence will be impossible and torturing... Then the Spirit of God answered me... Prayers... that is the major things a multi-dimensional reasoning being can do... in silence... Making good use of the Talk-active-ness...Think about this...

The nature of woman tends to lead them to usurp authority over man and take charge... You do not blame them, they are smart... they are the solution hub... they are correct most of the time... however; if they allow this to run, with the lack of vision and direction, the woman will ruin the very thing she was meant to proffer help and solution for. This is why; to birth this great smartness... women are to bring their wisdom forth through prayers... in silence!

This may seem longer route instead of simply telling the man what to do... (which is shorter and faster)... God enjoins woman to pray it through instead...

The woman is the 'PRAY-ER' of her husband and household... When a woman makes praying for her husband her sole responsibility, she gives birth to a very great man...

You do not need to know how to pray... The ability to pray is inherent in every woman…. If she can get to be silence... Her prayers will make the man... If she can be silence... All the smartness in her converged into prayers …Women will make great men on earth...

As a Life Coach, the Spirit of GOD taught us in our coaching program how to 'Gossip with JESUS'… just tell JESUS... just tell Him about it all... This is so homely and natural with women…Many outstanding miracles have been born through this! Think about this... 'Gossip with JESUS?'

'Gossip with JESUS'…
just tell JESUS...

just tell Him about it all…

This is so homely and natural with women…

The highest form of submission is...Prayer. You are smart... You know what... Yet gives it out to your man...This can only be done in silence...In prayers... In a submission to the one that is a chief in silence... The Holy Spirit... The silence mover... The silence shaker... The silence maker...

When a woman submits in silence... In prayers...Then GOD uses her to perfect the man... And the man becomes his best. It is not good for man to be alone... I will, therefore, make him a helpmeet for him...

The woman is the helpmeet for man... To equip the man to fulfil the mandate of the BLESSING... To be fruitful, multiply, replenish the earth, subdue it and have dominion... That is why the Bible says...He that finds a wife ... finds a good thing... and has obtained favour from the Lord...

The woman is equated to GOD's favour... Unmerited. Undeserved ... and effortless victory.

Because the smartness of the man is the woman! Therefore, what GOD has joined together... Let no man put asunder...

However, the woman needs a very conducive atmosphere to carry out her birthing responsibilities...

That is why the only mandate GOD gave a man is to love his wife...When you show affection towards a woman...She comes to you...However when you show love to a woman... She makes you... She sticks with you... And she makes you a great man...

Joy comes from what you know... Happiness comes from what you feel... In between, I believe and here it is... You need patience.

'Now the just shall live by faith; But if anyone draws back, My soul has no pleasure in him.' (Hebrews 10:36, NKJV).

Bible patience is being consistently and constantly standing on your belief of the finished work of JESUS CHRIST...irrespective of opposing circumstances.

Stay consistent ... Do not give up... The just shall live by faith...Faith takes what the grace has made available...

A woman can never do a good job all by herself... The woman was created to make man... When this is not gotten... And she 'lost' her husband... The woman turns to her son... Just any man to make... Reason for mother in law crisis...She failed in making her husband... Hence, she is trying this on her son... Some try it on their brothers... other women's husband..., their pastors... just any man available to them... Go back and make your husband...

> **if a man lacks wisdom and he is not empowered…**
>
> **check out his woman, she is not transferring her smartness and intuitions effectively unto him through prayers!**

The making of a man is in Silence … in Prayers… Channelling all of your smartness, intuition and instincts unto GOD in prayers. As you pray for your man… GOD fixes him! When you insist on talking and correcting and instructing your man because of your instinct and smartness, you harden him… However, when you go to GOD instead and lay all of the concerns to GOD in prayers, you soften and empowered your man to prosper.

Therefore, if your man is not empowered, check out his woman, she is not transferring the smartness and intuitions effectively unto him!

Your Notes . . .

The characteristics of the 1st woman, the offence of the woman and the redeemed woman... where are you (or your spouse) in all of these...

The 3rd Person in Marriage

THE GODLY

MARRIAGE

4. THE GODLY MARRIAGE··· (GOD + MAN + WOMAN)···

The Godly Marriage . . . (God + Man + Woman)

*T*he Godly Marriage is the combination of a man, a woman and GOD in action!

Man bringing to fore... Dominion / Authority; Vision /Direction; and Stability... Woman bringing to fore... Insights/ Smartness; Influence; and Beauty... The Spirit of marriage... strengthening man... and empowering woman… What a combination!

No man can exhibit all of these traits without the help of the Spirit of GOD!... So also, no woman can ever effectively use her smartness without her submission to the Spirit of GOD! The Spirit of oneness, GOD... Making man with foresight and enabling woman with insight!

THE GODLY MARRIAGE . . . (GOD + MAN + WOMAN)
This is the Godly marriage... There is no error in GOD!

Will you submit to the 3rd person in marriage today to get the best of you for your union? If not... You are short-changing your life, your family, your community and your generation!

Only in GOD... can man become that real man... Only in submitting to the Spirit of GOD ... can a man develop his GOD's given attributes of Dominion... Authority... Vision and Direction... Stability... Strength...

> *Without GOD, Man's authority will not withstand the smartness of the woman...*

Without GOD, Man's authority will not stand the smartness of the woman...

Man's direction will be questioned and flawed... Often this leads to man using his stability to bully the woman instead of shielding and support her... However... A man with supernaturally empowered traits... receive the submission of a woman naturally...

Similarly...Only in GOD can a woman's smartness be effectively harnessed for a goodly purpose...

An ungodly woman is a very dangerous tool for any man, family, community and people... Submitting to the Holy Spirit in silence...through prayers, will bring all her intuition for positive use... Only a praying woman can win her home...Her influence, when channelled through GOD and under a man's vision will birth great fruits... In all endeavours...

Behind a successful man. Is a woman: his mother, or wife, or girlfriend or a girl somewhere in the street...

73

Therefore, for a Godly Marriage... It is between a Man, a Woman and the third Person in Marriage... The Spirit of Marriage... GOD the Father. The three parties must contribute to the marriage... The man bringing Dominion /Authority; Vision/Direction... and Stability... The woman bringing in Smartness /Intuition; Influence... and Beauty... and The 3rd Person, GOD joining these two in harmony... as they both yield and align for His binding force.

Aligning with the Spirit of marriage is key to success in marriage...

An ungodly woman is a very dangerous tool for any man, family, community and people...

Submitting to the Holy Spirit in silence...through prayers, will bring all her intuition for positive use...

Quit trying to change your spouse... Knowing that we are all at different levels of yielded-ness to the Spirit of GOD... Focusing rather on your yielding to the Spirit... Will birth better relationship.

Love is a deliberate conscious decision... of believing the best of the object of love... You cannot give love if you have not partaken of it yourself... When you yield to the love of GOD...

When you allow GOD to fix and manage your weaknesses... It becomes easier for you to comprehend with other saints (especially your spouse) the height, the length, the width and the breadth... of love!

Until you are grounded in the love of CHRIST... This cannot happen...

Meanwhile... That is why ... Love himself is teaming with you... The oneness of GOD... Becoming the Spirit of marriage... So that it is practically impossible for any marriage not to work... Except a man/woman deliberately put it asunder... For what GOD has joined together ... Let no man put asunder...

Therefore, a Godly Marriage... is between a Man, a Woman and the third Person in Marriage... The Spirit of Marriage... GOD the Father.

Man or woman has a right on this earth... Because of their freely given will, hence can halt anything... Otherwise... Godly marriage will work any day, anytime, anywhere, under any circumstances... Amen...

.

Your Notes . . .

A Godly marriage is between a man, a woman and GOD... what is your take on this...

MANAGING CRISIS ... OF UNDERSTANDING MARRIAGE

Satan attacks everything that GOD values... And marriage is one of them, which has suffered a great deal of attack from the enemy...

"Then JESUS said to those Jews who believed Him, "if you abide in my word, you are my disciples indeed. And you shall know the truth, and the truth shall make you free." (John 8:31-32, NKJV)

Man has a will to choose on this earth... GOD gave every man and woman on this earth the honour of a will to choose... And it is what you choose that is permitted to happen to you.

[15]*"See, I have set before you today life and good, death and evil,*

[19]*I call heaven and earth as witnesses today against you, that I have set before you life and death, blessing and cursing; <u>therefore choose</u> life, that both you and your descendants may live;" (Deuteronomy 30:15, 19, NKJV)*

Choose marital bliss today... Choose the truth... Give no place to the Devil... For if you know the Truth, the Truth will set you free.

"Nor give place to the devil." (Ephesians 4:27 NKJV)

Satan attacks everything that GOD values... And marriage has suffered a great deal of attack from the enemy...

Resist the devil... Use your weapon of warfare...The name of JESUS...The blood of JESUS... Cast down imaginations and every high thing that stands in the way of CHRIST in your mind...

Satan focuses mainly on blindfolding the mind of men... So the light of the gospel will not shine on them. Cast this down... Rebuke the enemy over your marriage and marital destiny.

Many are attacked by way of a wrong understanding of what marriage is... Many are wrongly informed of the characteristics of the man and woman... many are opinionated based on their experiences and past pain... all of these standing in the way of their marital bliss... However, the good news is: GOD says we should cast down all these imaginations and wrong beliefs, so the light of the Gospel, which is the image of CHRIST might shine upon us.

[3]"For though we walk in the flesh, we do not war according to the flesh. [4]For the weapons of our warfare are not carnal but mighty in God for pulling down strongholds, [5]casting down arguments and every high thing that exalts itself against the knowledge of God, bringing every thought into captivity to the obedience of CHRIST, [6]and being ready to punish all disobedience when your obedience is fulfilled." (2 Corinthians 10:3-6, NKJV)

Finally... Submit to the truth... It is the truth that you know that will set you free... Let the Truth on the foundational Truth on Marriage; The characteristics of the man and the woman, The 3rd Person in Marriage and what a Godly marriage is ... guide and set you free...

[31]"Then JESUS said to those Jews who believed Him, "if you abide in my word, you are my disciples indeed. [32]And you shall know the truth, and the truth shall make you free." (John 8:31-32, NKJV)

It is you continuing … abiding in GOD's word, that you are His disciples indeed, and that is when the Truth will be revealed unto you… And this Truth will set you free… The key is 'ABID'NG'… 'CONTINUING' in GOD's word!

Ask yourself... Am I the man described above ... Am I short... Am I the offence woman...Am I the redeemed woman... And begin to yield to the Spirit of GOD...

Today... The Spirit of oneness... In your marriage will speak for you... We speak peace over every storm in your marriage in YESHUA HAMASHIACH Name, Amen... Go... And return with your testimonies in YESHUA name, Amen

Your Notes . . .

What measures are you taking to ensure your relationship is in alignment with GOD's Truth...

The 3rd Person in Marriage

series...

THE PREPARATIONS

pst tomowo

THE PREPARATIONS...

THE PREPARATIONS IN MARRIAGE . . .

*T*he Preparations ... of The 3rd Person in Marriage Series ... is focusing mainly at the preparatory stage in Marriage... targeting how and why the need for preparation and the specific preparations needed for successful marital relationship.

What we see today as the crisis in marriages are not born from the immediate two or so years of marriage... they are deep-seated in our upbringing... the very core of our makeup. Many of the difficulties and incompatibilities in relationships are because of ill-upbringing. The Spirit of GOD began to nudge me as He exposes to me the need to prepare for marriage from young. ... Or else future failures will be inevitable.

Even if this preparatory stage exposes many flaws in your characters, the intention is to help reveal the very reasons behind the raw materials you brought into your marriage, hence seeing how and why your marriage is working or not working.

As we encouraged earlier, have an open mind, let the Holy Spirit show you an X-ray of your personality and that of your spouse, so you might see what and what to continue with and what to improve upon or be done away with... in your relationship.

We will be looking into the need and why ... Preparing the boy for marriage; Preparing the girl for marriage; Raising a Godly man; Raising a Godly woman; Who actually am I? and Engaging the 3rd person in marriage in preparations...

Having saddled with the basic understanding of Marriage in the previous chapter, we will now be looking at the nitty-gritty of why and what to prepare for in marriage. ...

Let us do this ...

PREPARING THE BOY FOR MARRIAGE

The 3rd Person in Marriage

5. PREPARING THE BOY FOR MARRIAGE ···

PROTECTING THE SEED OF MANHOOD IN THE BOY CHILD...

*P*reparing the boy for marriage... protecting the seed of manhood...

Every child is born with all the full potential of who he should be... The basic characteristics: Dominion and Authority, Vision and Direction... and Stability were deposited into every baby boy born into the world. However, in the course of upbringing, if these traits are not nurtured and well preserved, they could be lost and result in mere figurehead males we see in the world today.

Protecting the seed of manhood is the sole responsibility of every parent, caretaker, community and nation at large. Looking into the crisis in the world today, it is glaring that the full potential Father figures, well-groomed men with full capacity to operate is lacking.

Many men are so lost they dropped deep into identity confusion. These all do not start from a day, this can be traced back to the boy child. Protecting the seed of manhood in the boy child is the guarantee of future authorities, directions and stability in all sphere of life.

The basic characteristics: Dominion and Authority, Vision and Direction… and Stability were deposited into every baby boy born into the world.

The Lord created man and woman and blessed them… to be fruitful, multiply… and have dominion!

"Then God blessed them, and God said to them, "be fruitful and multiply; fill the earth and subdue it; have dominion over the fish of the sea, over the birds of the air, and over every living thing that moves on the earth." (Genesis 1:28, NKJV)

After the creation, when GOD saw that all He created was good… He rested on the seventh day…For completion not for tiredness… The man was created complete at birth… managing this boy child is where the error comes from.

"Thus the heavens and the earth, and all the host of them,

were finished. And on the seventh day, God ended his work which he had done, and he rested on the seventh day from all his work which he had done. Then God blessed the seventh day and sanctified it, because in it He rested from all his work which God had created and made." (Genesis 2:1-3, NKJV)

For continuity of the completion in creation, GOD put the remnant of his Spirit in marriage ... For He desires Godly children...

"But did he not make them one, having a remnant of the Spirit? And why one? He seeks Godly offspring. Therefore take heed to your Spirit, and let none deal treacherously with the wife of his youth." (Malachi 2:15, NKJV)

So... for everyone born into the world. The seed of fruitfulness and completeness was deposited in them... except the enemy crept in on this...For he is a thief to steal, kill and destroy...

"The thief does not come except to steal, and to kill, and to destroy. I have come that they may have life, and that they may have it more abundantly." (John 10:10 NKJV)

Where then is the seed of manhood deposited at birth in the boy-child...How are they losing it...Who is taking them away from them? **When the boy loses his manhood...He grows up to become an ordinary male...Or becomes a perverted male... This is the target of the enemy...**

However, when a boy child is protected...growing up into real men will be inevitable... The Bible says *'Train up a child in the way he should go, and when he is old he will not departs from it...' (Proverbs 22:6, NKJV)*

"Foolishness is bound up in the heart of a child; the rod of correction will drive it far from him." (Proverbs 22:15, NKJV)

This is the reason for this chapter ... The preparatory stage in marriage ... Preparing the boy for marriage...

In preparing the boy for marriage, let us take a quick look at the overview of the man in marriage...

The three basic elements of the man in marriage...

1. Dominion and Authority...

GOD gave Adam dominion mandate...

"Then God blessed them, and GOD said to them, "be fruitful and multiply; fill the earth and subdue it; have dominion over the fish of the sea, over the birds of the air, and over every living thing that moves on the earth." (Genesis 1:28 NKJV)

2. Vision and Direction...

GOD gave Adam instructions of what to do and what not to do in the garden... Man is the one with the vision, direction...Man has foresight. ..

[15]*"Then the Lord God took the man and put him in the garden of Eden to tend and keep it.* [16]*And the Lord God commanded the man, saying, "of every tree of the garden you may freely eat;* [17]*but of the tree of the knowledge of good and evil you shall not eat, for in the day that you eat of it you shall surely die." (Genesis 2:15-17, NKJV)*

3. Stability...

Physical strength ...Roughness...Toughness...No hormonal changes ... No monthly cycle... Stability... To sustain the weaker vessel made not as stable... Men are wired to be stable... Not for selfish display... It is to sustain every other thing that is not as stable...

[21]*"And the Lord God caused a deep sleep to fall on Adam, and he slept, and he took one of his ribs, and closed up the flesh in its place.* [24]*Therefore a man shall leave his father and mother and be joined to his wife, and they shall become one flesh." (Genesis 2:21, 24 NKJV)*

These above-listed seeds are delicate... They can be easily lost... Hence a need to consciously protect them... especially while the boy child is growing up.

Take a second look at a little boy; they start to exhibit these traits until the un-informed adults start to kill these traits in them. The Authority and Dominion can come in form of rebelliousness to the norms, Vision and Directions may show up as wanting things done their way... Stability may show up as been uncaring and indifferent to others...

When one does not understand these traits, many caretakers correct the boy child insisting on the desires of the parents and caretakers, instead of insisting on the right way... The Bible says 'train up a child in the way he should go'... not just in any other opinion...

'Train up a child in the way he should go, and when he is old he will not departs from it...' (Proverbs 22:6 NKJV)

Many parents use the children as a tool of vengeance to their spouse's offences, many use the oppression from their parents and vent on their children… However, in the course of this diverse ill-treatment, the seed of manhood is destroyed in the boy child. Understanding these traits and the importance of these traits should propel parents and caretakers to nurture them, promote them, and encourage their expression in the boy-child. Encouraging the boy-child to make decisions, to stand by decisions, to be stable in crisis… not been too fast to rescue him from the simple age-related crisis of life… Doing these, help to protect the seed of manhood in them… and their generation will thank you for this.

> *Encouraging the boy-child to make decisions, to stand by his decisions, to be stable… not quick to rescue them from simple age-related crisis… helps to protect the seed of manhood in them…*

SOME BIBLICAL EXAMPLES …

Let us see some Biblical examples of how the seed of manhood in the boy child is expressed and protected:

JESUS CHRIST OUR LORD... AS A BOY-CHILD...

He was found among scholars deliberating on issues of life. This was expressing His authority and dominion; He went about his heavenly father's business … Vision/direction; He subjected to his parents afterwards… Stability…

[41]*"His parents went to Jerusalem every year at the feast of the Passover.* [42]*And when he was twelve years old, they went up to Jerusalem according to the custom of the feast.*

[43-45]*When they had finished the days, as they returned, the boy JESUS lingered behind in Jerusalem. And Joseph and his mother did not know it; but supposing him to have been in the company, they went a day's journey, and sought him among their relatives and acquaintances. So when they did not find him, they returned to Jerusalem, seeking him.*

[46-47]*Now so it was that after three days they found him in the temple, sitting in the midst of the teachers, both listening to them and asking them questions. And all who heard him were astonished at his understanding and answers.*

[48]*So when they saw him, they were amazed; and his mother said to him, "Son, why have you done this to us? Look, your father and I have sought you anxiously."*

[49-50]*And he said to them, "why did you seek me?* <u>*Did you not know that I must be about my father's business?"*</u> *But they did not understand the statement which he spoke to them.*

[51.] <u>*Then he went down with them and came to Nazareth, and was subject to them,*</u> *but his mother kept all these things in her heart.* [52] <u>*and JESUS increased in wisdom and stature, and in favor with God and men."*</u> *(Luke 2:41-52 NKJV)*

The boy child exhibits these traits often, '...Did you not know that I must be about my father's business?'... 'I'm in charge here'... 'I will take good care of you mummy'... 'This is my dad's car, do not touch it'...

When you see this, it is because they are expressing their GOD's given traits of Dominion and Authority... As much as they are to be well-groomed, corrected, and aligned, care must be taken not to destroy that seed of manhood in them...

From the above scriptures, they entreated him mildly ... and he subjected to His parents and '...then he went down with them and came to Nazareth, and was subject to them.' (Luke 2:51)

> *As much as they are to be well-groomed, corrected, and aligned, care must be taken not to destroy that seed of manhood in them...*

'...But His mother kept all these things in her heart'... She did not insist and destroy this seed, she ponders on it, nurturing it...

As caretakers, while it is still very right to nurture the boy child from rebelliousness and danger... care should be taken not to damage these delicate traits when you see them in manifestation... rather, they should be promoted, encouraged and given opportunities to be expressed within the context of decency and uprightness...

DAVID... AS A BOY A AND YOUNG MAN...

Always in the bush caring for his father's sheep... (Authority and dominion −responsible). He challenged goliath for insulting his GOD... (Vision and direction). He submitted to King Saul... (Stability).

Let us take a closer look at this:

David expressing authority and dominion challenged Goliath, a prey against his GOD's property... the Israelites.

[23]*"Then as he talked with them, there was the champion, the philistine of Gath, Goliath by name, coming up from the armies of the Philistines; and he spoke according to the same words. So David heard them.*

[26.] *Then David spoke to the men who stood by him, saying, "what shall be done for the man who kills this Philistine and takes away the reproach from Israel? For who is this uncircumcised Philistine, that he should defy the armies of the living God?" (1 Samuel 17:23, 26 NKJV).*

David expressing a sense of responsibility... his dominion and authority traits... The elder brother took it as rebelliousness and pride...

"Now Eliab his oldest brother heard when he spoke to the men;

and Eliab's anger was aroused against David, and he said, "why did you come down here? And with whom have you left those few sheep in the wilderness? I know your pride and the insolence of your heart, for you have come down to see the battle." *(1 Samuel 17:28 NKJV)*

David expressing Stability… Pillar… Protection. He followed the directives of King Saul… as he also rested on his faith in GOD…

[34]*"But David said to Saul, "your servant used to keep his father's sheep, and when a lion or a bear came and took a lamb out of the flock,* [35]*I went out after it and struck it, and delivered the lamb from its mouth; and when it arose against me, I caught it by its beard, and struck and killed it.*

[36]*Your servant has killed both lion and bear; and this uncircumcised Philistine will be like one of them, seeing he has defied the armies of the living GOD." Moreover,* [37]*David said, "the Lord, who delivered me from the paw of the lion and from the paw of the bear, he will deliver me from the hand of this Philistine." And Saul said to David, "go, and the Lord be with you!"* *(1 Samuel 17:34-37, NKJV)*

THE ROLES OF CARETAKERS IN PREPARING THE BOY CHILD…

In protecting the seed of manhood in the boy-child…, the father, mother, teacher, community, peers and the church… everyone is a stakeholder. We all have a part to play in this. Let us see the different responsibilities as follow:

THE BOY'S FATHER...

This is the very first picture a boy sees and learns from...If it is wrong here... It will almost automatically affect the seed of manhood in the boy-child...

Everything the father does, his actions, his in-actions, the way he treats his mother, the way he relates to the public... everything he does is what the boy-child sees first as to how a man should be.

If the father is Blessed, the boy will be raised well, however, if the father is in life struggle of any kind, financially, mentally, socially, abusive, or oppressed by the wife... the boy replicates these in his life

A boy does not have control over who his father or father figure is while growing up... however, if you are exposed wrongly due to a wrong treated father figure, it is important to acknowledge this and seek to deal with this deficit in your life.

Take a close look at your father figure as a boy, does he possess the basic traits of Dominion and Authority, Vision and Direction, and Stability... or does he lack in these traits ...

A boy does not have control over who his father or father figure is while growing up... however, if you are exposed wrongly due to a wrong treated father figure, it is important to acknowledge this and seek to

98

deal with this deficit in your life. Or else, you will carry this baggage with you in future relationships.

Fathers and father figures must go the extra mile to reflect and train up the boy in their care. Paying close attention to the boy, consciously revealing to him what and what is expected of a man in different issues of life. Even if the father is a deficit in some, he should be truthful and expose his boys to learn from great men who possess these traits. Raising a boy child and protecting the seed of manhood is key to a glorious future generation. It is a great responsibility...

THE BOY'S MOTHER...

This is the very first teacher of the boy child... If the mother is operating under 'offence' instead of 'redemption' as described in earlier chapters of understanding the woman in marriage ... She will destroy the seed of manhood in the boy-child... She will suppress him with her smartness... Making decisions for him always... Giving a picture that woman takes the lead at home... Causing him to lose confidence in himself and lacking self-worth.

Today, the rate of single-parenting is increasing, many homes are run by women; as much as the condition might be unavoidable, when a woman solely raise a boy, indirectly, she will kill the seed of manhood in that boy, unless of course, the woman is knowledgeable and deliberately pose the boy with a male figure to learn from.

As the first teacher of a boy, care must be taken not to push the control too far. A woman's smartness will flaw a natural adult man, anyway anytime, talk less of a mere boy…. Hence, care must be taken, not to unleash all of woman's 'smartness' on the boy child…

There must be conscious effort to promote the boy to make decisions, stand by his decisions and follow through with his visions and directions and promoting stability in the face of challenges.

> *A woman's smartness will flaw a natural adult man, anyway anytime, talk less of a mere boy….*
>
> *Hence, care must be taken, not to unleash all of woman's 'smartness' on the boy child…*

Secondly, the mother must show an example of what a Godly lady should be like with a man, by showing submission, being a helpmeet indeed and influencing rather than usurping authority., … especially in her dealings with the boy's father. This unspoken character becomes the very core of how the boy views man and woman in his relationships later in life.

When a boy is raised by an offence-based mother, the boy becomes talkative, sissy, weak to take charge, weak to be in control, and unstable… resulting in aggression and prone to abuse due to lack of his manhood - 'ego'.

The popular 'EGO' displayed by many men are reactions to their lack and destroyed seed of manhood'…

Take a very close look at your mother or mother figure as a boy, did she operates as 'an offence woman' described above or as 'a redeemed woman'? Her character will portray how you view and what you invariably expect from women in life afterwards. If you see any deficit in this … own up to it and seek to address it. These are the root cause of many ills we see in world marriages today.

There may not be a perfect upbringing, however, assessing your upbringing for these deficits will reveal the degree of damage and how much is needed to fix them… Fixing this root cause will help not only your spouse, children and society… it will also help you as a man!

> **The popular 'EGO' displayed by many men are reactions to their lack and destroyed seed of manhood'…**

THE SOCIETAL INFLUENCE...

The society has a great influence on protecting or destroying the seed of manhood in the boy child. The new-age culture, the society correctness, the ways of life of the 'stars' and celebrities, all of these inform the views and perception of the boy child. If the society you are brought up in has adversely affected the way you view marriage, … If you have lost the seed of manhood in you, all hope is not lost… Are you willing to change, then, GOD can fix even this for you!

'For with GOD, nothing shall be impossible'. (Luke 1:37, KJV)

Like the world of the internet today... The community culture... the 'society correctness'... the generally accepted norms today can greatly influence the boy-child.

PEER PRESSURE...

What other kids are doing... And how they relate... can equally take a tone on what a boy does or not. This is also an expression of societal influence. There are many positively promoted clubs for young boys today in communities, search to see if you can assess one for your boy child... where he can relate with Godly likeminded age group of his.

THE CHURCH...

This is the last place that the seed of manhood could be protected... Encouraging the boy child to engage in church activities of his age... not adult class... There are many biblical ways taught in the church.

The Church is a good place to bridge the gaps and mend the vacuum of lack of father figure, poor mother's influence, societal influences and peer pressure. Many churches have age-related and targeted programmes that will promote many great figures from the scriptures capable of protecting and nurturing the seed of manhood in man. This should be taken advantage of, even if you believe you are doing well as a parent.

THE ABUSIVE AND STRESSED MARRIAGE...

Abusive and stressed marriages are common today... the reason we are learning more on marriage.

When there is an abusive or stressed marriage, the two principal parties (husband and wife)... become engrossed into their affairs and forgets that the children are worse hit in the situation.

> *Understand that every child is a gift... you do not own them...rather seeing yourself as a caretaker focusing on raising a greater future...*

Children dragged into the problem, abused, accused or used as tools of abuse between the couples... all of these bring a load of negative impact on the children. Many children have this as their realities today... so sad! Many do not even get to know their biological parents and are at the mercy of some uncaring caretakers or foster parents...

Understanding that every child is a gift... And you do not own them...rather seeing yourself as a caretaker ...Focusing on raising a greater future... Where there is no ideal fatherhood to emulate...Or redeemed mother to help protect the seed of manhood; It will be a blessing if you expose your boy child to learn about great men... Even if not directly..., if not possible physically, let it be done indirectly through books, motivating movies, and stories...This will help future relationships...

Your Notes . . .

What are the roles you can take to protect the seed of manhood in the boy child in your care...

Your Notes . . .

How can you prepare a boy child in an abusive and challenged family setting...

The 3rd Person in Marriage

PREPARING THE GIRL FOR MARRIAGE

6. PREPARING THE GIRL FOR MARRIAGE…

RAISING THE HELPMEET IN A GIRL CHILD…

As described above… every child is born with all the full potential of who he or she should be…

The Lord created man and woman and blessed them… To be fruitful and multiply… Hence the helpmeet is already embedded in every girl child.

"27So God created man in His own image; in the image of God He created him; male and female He created them. 28Then GOD blessed them, and GOD said to them, "be fruitful and multiply; fill the earth and subdue it; have dominion over the fish of the sea, over the birds of the air, and over every living thing that moves on the earth." (Genesis 1:27-28 NKJV)

GOD saw that all he created was good... GOD rested on the 7th day... For completion not for tiredness...

"Thus the heavens and the earth, and all the host of them, were finished. ²And on the seventh day, God ended his work which he had done, and he rested on the seventh day from all his work which he had done. ³Then God blessed the seventh day and sanctified it, because in it He rested from all his work which God had created and made." (Genesis 2:1-3, NKJV)

GOD put the remnant of his Spirit in marriage … For the desire of Godly children...

> **Every girl child has in her the completion of what it takes to be a helpmeet for her future husband...**

"But did he not make them one, having a remnant of the Spirit? And why one? He seeks Godly offspring. Therefore take heed to your Spirit, and let none deal treacherously with the wife of his youth." (Malachi 2:15, NKJV).

So... For everyone born into the world... The seed of fruitfulness and completeness is in them... Except the enemy creeps in on it... For he is a thief to steal, kill and destroy...

"The thief does not come except to steal, and to kill, and to destroy. I have come that they may have life, and that they may have it more abundantly." (John 10:10, NKJV)

Therefore, every girl child has in her the completion of what it takes to be a helpmeet for her future husband... The basic characteristics of a woman... The Smartness and Intuition; Influence; and Beauty... are inherent in every girl child...

Woman... The helpmeet...

Let us look at the characteristics of the woman as described earlier on Understanding as follows:

THE INSTINCT... SMARTNESS...

Created to be a helpmeet, a solution hub, the woman endowed to see at multiple levels to proffer all possible outcome for a project or mission... She was placed by the forbidden tree at the Garden of Eden... she sure got three reasons why she had to taste of the tree... Smartness, Instinct...

> *The basic characteristics of a woman... The Smartness and Intuition; Influence; and Beauty... are inherent in every girl child...*

And when the woman saw that the tree was good for food, and that it was pleasant to the eyes, and a tree to be desired to make one wise, she took of the fruit thereof, and did eat, and gave also to her husband with her, and he did eat.' (Genesis 3:6 KJV)

Naturally, the girl child will always come up with many suggestions to many things, depicted by her many questions, take-activeness and explorations... However, as with the first woman, Eve, this smartness must be well-groomed and channelled into a right

110

course of vision and direction, or else it will become a cause of confusion, chaos and offence… With this smartness, a girl child must be nurtured early on the need to align with laid down authority, vision, and direction…

Curbing usurping authority, not insisting on their ways, and talkativeness is key in preparing a girl child for marriage… If these are not dealt with at the young age, the girl may grow up as an 'offence woman' bringing solutions to evil places…

> *Curbing usurping authority, not insisting on their ways, and talkativeness is key in preparing a girl child for marriage…*

Helping the girl-child to exercise smartness in dealing with issues… is a good thing.

THE INFLUENCE…

The very second inherent trait of a woman is Influence… woman with the multi-dimensional way of reasoning and approaching things, she surely will influence even the strongest-willed man around her… especially if the man is in love with her. Eve gave Adam the fruit to eat; Samson eventually gave in to Delilah's pressure and revealed the secret of his power to her…

"And when the woman saw that the tree was good for food, and that it was pleasant to the eyes, and a tree to be desired to make one wise, <u>she took of the fruit thereof, and did eat, and gave also unto her husband with her; and he did eat</u>." (Genesis 3:6, KJV)

111

Pranks, tricks, pretence, lies and deceptions are very common with a girl child... these are some expression of their multi-dimensional reasoning... that girl... a lot is going on in her brain... she will try out many ways to get your attention...

Encouraging the girl-child to practice submission to authority is key in preparing her for marriage. Introducing submission instead of usurping authority...

Allowing a girl to have her way always is a RED FLAG and indication of raising an 'offence woman'... This must be discouraged... Rather, dialogue and reasoning to garner submission should be promoted... This of course is not to oppress the girl child or abuse her...

Encouraging the girl-child to practice submission to authority is key in preparing her for marriage.

Introducing submission instead of usurping authority...

Many society and tradition have resulted in suppressing the girl child to the extent of denying them rights to education, health, welfare and the goods of life... No matter how much you try to suppress a girl... her smartness and intuition will still be intact... this, however, may be perverted.

It is therefore important instead to nurture these traits for good use... Promoting influence instead of usurping authority by encouraging dialogue…The emphasis is to promote dialogue instead of allowing her insisting on her right…

Discouraging her from been authoritative … Promoting influence instead...

THE BEAUTY...

Beauty to a woman is beyond the physical look… Inherent in every girl is the skills, abilities and desires to present and package herself in the best stylish and beautiful way possible… Beauty also goes with flirting… Every woman is endowed with the ability to flirt… seducing and flaunting her looks for the attention of the opposite sex. (even when she pretends she is innocent!).

> *Every woman is endowed with the ability to flirt…*
>
> *Parading and flaunting her looks for the attention of the opposite sex. (even when she pretends she is innocent!).*

This is seen in every girl child unless there is an attack on her.

Forever, man will always be fascinated with the beauty of a woman.

Have you wonder why women are so pretty, shapely, soft –talking, with a sweet voice, soft face, cool smile, waist twisting, slim arms, … think about that… BEAUTY… this is a trait endowed every woman.

[22]And the rib, which the Lord God had taken from man, made he a woman, and brought her unto the man. [23]and Adam said: "This is now <u>bone of my bones</u> and flesh of my flesh; <u>she shall be called woman because she was taken out of man."</u> (Genesis 2:22-23 NKJV).

In preparing a girl child for marriage... there are a lot of things to bring to fore:

Showing the girl-child self-management; Beautification routine and keeping up with personal branding; Home management and diligence and Protection of the girl child from evil...

- SELF-MANAGEMENT FOR THE GIRL CHILD...

Showing the girl child self-management is key to preparing her for marriage. How to talk, how to pose, how to carry oneself in public, how to present soft, naïve, chaste and decent... Many churches and some cultures and communities do have organized schemes that girls and teenagers can engage in to promote this...

- BEAUTIFICATION ROUTINE AND KEEPING UP WITH PERSONAL BRANDING...

Beautification routine and personal branding are equally important in preparing a girl child for marriage. Encouraging a girl to work on her beautification routine, personal hygiene, and personal branding is key. Many resources can be assessed for this. On the internet and locally. When you encourage a girl child to

114

engage in this, it helps them channel their multi-dimensional energy into good use. Beautification and personal branding also boost self-confidence and shield from the external oppression in the world today.

- HOME MANAGEMENT AND DILIGENCE...

Home management and diligence require a lot of skills, time and tolerance... Hence very easy for women. Love and caring are natural with women... That is why GOD did not make it a law for them...

Home management... is diverse and require a lot of attention ... making the multi-dimension wired being the more suitable for it. A woman can do several things at the same time, cooking, doing the laundry, making a call, fixing the kids' school assignment, putting them to bed,... yet, still ready to attend to her husband later... (Did I say after both the husband and wife got home from work)... many men on the order side, will be so tired, confused, and unfit if asked to manage the home for only a day...

In the Book of Esther... It was revealed that to be a queen, there must be preparations ... could this be a type and a shadow of what should be for every Godly woman.

They prepare the girls for 'queenship' for a whole year...

"And let the king appoint officers in all the provinces of his kingdom, that they may gather all the beautiful young virgins to Shushan the citadel, into the women's quarters, under the custody
115

of Hegai the king's eunuch, custodian of the women. And let beauty preparations be given them." (Esther 2:3 NKJV).

"Each young woman's turn came to go in to King Ahasuerus after <u>she had completed twelve months' preparation,</u> according to the regulations for the women, for thus were the days of their preparation apportioned: <u>six months with oil of myrrh,</u> and <u>six months with perfumes and preparations for beautifying women</u>." (Esther 2:12, NKJV)

The girl child is to learn the following: How to talk...How to flirt...How to manage a man... How to keep a home... How to keep children among others.

Men are created to function... with a help... Be that help...

Men's roughness...Men's lack of insights... Men's lack of attention to details... Men's big goal and vision... Men's acquisition ... Dominion ... All of these require ... Some help, the woman is equipped for such... Expose the girl child to this early...

Creativity...Hard works... Not promoting equality with men...Rather promoting the right of a girl child... As the girl child has the right to the basics of life...Education, Civilization, Health, Right to express herself ... Socialization... Modernization... As we preserve the elements of the helpmeet in her... She will become better for it...

A woman with these skills and traits ...are more tolerant, happier, calmer, and accommodating...

PROTECTION OF THE GIRL CHILD FROM EVIL…

Finally, it is the responsibility of caretakers to protect the girl child from preying evil eyes in the world… The naivety and innocence a girl child exhibits is oftentimes very attractive… This has lured many evil people to attack and defile the girl child… **The caretakers must see to it that the innocence of the girl child is protected… This responsibility must be taken seriously.**

> *The naivety and innocence a girl child exhibits is oftentimes very attractive…*
>
> *This has lured many evil people to attack and defile the girl child...*
>
> *She should be protected from this!*

Ensuring the basic signs to watch out for in evil people should be well spelt out and made public in the family… such as unnecessary fondness, wrong familiarities, unsupervised attention with male adults, reluctance towards anyone…

Young girls are very vulnerable; caretakers are to ensure that they are protected… Many schools and churches have programmes for this, however, in addition to what is learnt outside, the family must promote the value of the 'princess' and protect her from been defiled and unduly taken advantage of…

Encouraging the girl child to communicate … especially with the mother may be helpful. Caretakers must also be very vigilant for any usual attitude and behaviours of the girl child towards any

117

adult. When she says she does not like someone, please do not force her on him or her... That may be the only clue to a journey with an abusive adult.

Praying that GOD empowers the caretakers of the girl child to nurture and protect the GOD's given precious gifts (solution hubs) to the world.

Behind every successful man is a woman... his mother, or wife, or mistress... or a woman somewhere in the street.

A girl child well-groomed and nurtured is a BLESSING not only to her future husband and children, she is also a BLESSING to her parents, parents-in-law, community, market place and the world at large. Behind every successful man is a woman... his mother, or wife, or mistress... or a woman somewhere in the street.

The smartness and intuition in woman, if well-groomed, can birth the best of the best in life. The influence can melt any stony heart... The Beauty can captivate and make gladden any soul... Therefore, together, let us raise the so much needed helpmeets in the world today.

Many women are victims of abuse, rape, oppression and slavery today... So many we simply cannot deny this... If this is you, or your spouse... There is hope in CHRIST JESUS... what you need is HEALING... not revenge or repay... The pains, damage and hurt

118

caused cannot be reversed by mere revenge or repay. **There are a lot of professionals, specialists and experts that deal with issues like this... you are encouraged to seek help from them... In addition to this, please allow JESUS heal you...** This is the sure way. Irrespective of the degree of wholeness or brokenness, ... if you allow CHRIST to heal you... you will be healed and free from all the pains and damages.

'If the SON therefore shall make you free, ye shall free indeed.' (John 8:36, KJV)

Your Notes . . .

What are the roles you are taking in preparing the girl child in your care for marriage...

Your Notes . . .

How are you protecting the girl child in your care... from evil persons around you...

The 3rd Person in Marriage

RAISING A

GODLY MAN

7. RAISING A GODLY MAN ···

PRESERVING THE MUCH NEEDED FATHERHOOD…

*P*reserving the fatherhood… Raising a Godly man…

"Help, Lord, for the Godly man ceases! For the faithful disappear from among the sons of men." (Psalms 12:1, NKJV)

Why a Godly man… Though marriage is to be lived here on this earth… The outcome of it is beyond this world…

'We give thanks to GOD, and the father of our Lord JESUS CHRIST, praying always for you,' (Colossians 1:3, KJV).

[14]*"For this reason I bow my knees to the father of our Lord JESUS CHRIST,* [15]*Of whom the whole family in heaven and earth is named," (Ephesians 3:14-15, KJV)*

The result of marriage …, which is family, transcends beyond this world… GOD drops a heavenly touch in every marriage …The oneness of GOD…The Spirit of marriage …So that every offspring might be first and foremost Godly…

 "But did he not make them one, having a remnant of the Spirit? And why one? He seeks Godly offspring. Therefore take heed to your Spirit, and let none deal treacherously with the wife of his youth." (Malachi 2:15, NKJV)

For this reason, shall a man leave his father and mother, and shall cleave to his wife… And the two shall become one flesh…

> **GOD drops a heavenly touch in every marriage …The oneness of GOD…The Spirit of marriage …So that every offspring might be first and foremost Godly…**

23 "And Adam said: "This is now bone of my bones and flesh of my flesh; she shall be called woman, because she was taken out of man." 24 Therefore a man shall leave his father and mother and be joined to his wife, and they shall become one flesh." (Genesis 2:23-24, NKJV)

'Husbands love your wife as your selves… Just as CHRIST love the church, this is a great mystery… But I speak of CHRIST and the church' "This is a great mystery, but I speak concerning CHRIST and the church." (Ephesians 5:32, NKJV)

There is a need for understanding of the person of the woman…So the man can relate well with them…So that their prayers are not hindered!

"Husbands, likewise, dwell with them with understanding, giving honor to the wife, as to the weaker vessel, and as being heirs

together of the grace of life, that your prayers may not be hindered." (1 peter 3:7, NKJV)

The success of a marriage depends on the parties involved...The man...The woman... GOD... GOD is constant. He supplies the oneness. However, there must be an alignment of the other parties with GOD, for Him to effectively carry out His part...

"Draw near to God and He will draw near to you. Cleanse your hands, you sinners; and purify your hearts, you double-minded." (James 4:8 NKJV)

In this chapter, we are looking at the alignment of the man with GOD...Without your alignment; you can never be the fullest of what you are created for... As we said earlier, let this step be the standard for you, and help you see how much you are aligned with the manual, or see what and what needs to be added unto you.

WHO ACTUALLY IS A MAN...

In the understanding stage, we learnt of the three basic characteristics of the man in marriage ... Authority... Dominion. GOD made Adam have dominion. He named all of GOD's creatures... including the woman. Vision and direction... GOD gave Adam the do's and the don'ts... and Stability... Adam made strong, stable, without cycles..., etc.

All of these are seed deposited in every boy-child... However, they need to be nurtured in line with GOD's will...For their full manifestation. Unfortunately, these cannot be bought in the market... gyms, nor taught in the schools... they are endowed by the inspiration of the Almighty.

Without this endowment, man becomes a bully... using his physical strength to oppress the very person he is supposed to protect and nurture!

Let us recall the three foundational truth on marriage... Adam created as male and female... Complete and Perfect! The woman was removed from man... hence... Man and woman become incomplete and different... and GOD Almighty is the 3rd person in a marriage ... He joins them in the union...

> **_Without Divine endowment, man becomes a bully... using his physical strength to oppress the very person he is supposed to love, protect and nurture!_**

There is a myth out there that women rule the world... GOD did not render man useless... because of the woman... Lack of understanding has caused all the confusion in the world today...

Moreover, the enemy targets mainly the seed of manhood, to destroy man and all he represents! There is, therefore, a need for the restoration of the Seed of Manhood in the males today. This however cannot be possible without the endowment by the Holy Spirit. **The empowered man is called the Godly Man.** The Godly Man represents the fullness of what GOD deposits in Man for His Glory!

127

How then do we raise a Godly man...Needed for success in marriage...

Let us see the rendition here in Ephesians 5:22-33

[22] "Wives, submit to your own husbands, as to the Lord.

[23-24.] For the husband is head of the wife, as also CHRIST is head of the church;

And he is the saviour of the body. Therefore, just as the church is subject to CHRIST, so let the wives be to their own husbands in everything.

[25.] Husbands, love your wives, just as CHRIST also loved the church and gave himself for her,

[26-27] That he might sanctify and cleanse her with the washing of water by the word, that he might present her to himself a glorious church, not having spot or wrinkle or any such thing, but that she should be Holy and without blemish.

[28-29] So husbands ought to love their own wives as their own bodies; he who loves his wife loves himself. For no one ever hated his own flesh, but nourishes and cherishes it, just as the Lord does the church.

[30] For we are members of his body, of his flesh and of his bones.

[31] "for this reason a man shall leave his father and mother and be joined to his wife, and the two shall become one flesh."

32This is a great mystery, but I speak concerning CHRIST and the church.

33Nevertheless let each one of you in particular so love his own wife as himself, and let the wife see that she respects her husband."
(Ephesians 5:22-33, NKJV)

From the above scriptures, we shall be seeing some fundamental points as the Holy Spirit reveals the expected virtues of a Godly man and a Godly Woman.

THE QUALITIES OF A GODLY MAN...

I. HUSBAND IS THE HEAD OF THE WIFE...

The Husband is the head of the family, (It is not a man as head of all women... It is husband over his wife)! ... verses 23-24.

23-24For the husband is head of the wife, as also CHRIST is head of the church; And he is the saviour of the body. Therefore, just as the church is subject to CHRIST, so let the wives be to their own husbands in everything'.

.... As CHRIST is the head of the church...Taking on the name, the authority, the goal, the vision, the direction. JESUS as the saviour of the body... The head of the church! Protector, shield, deliverer. This is engaging the stability trait in the man!

In a team, there is always a leader... Husband is the head, the leader of the wife and family. This is what the manual says...

II. HUSBAND LOVES YOUR WIFE...

... Just as CHRIST loves the church...

[25.]'*husbands, love your wives, just as CHRIST also loved the church and gave himself for her,'* verse 25

This is a sacrificial giving of oneself to the wife. '<u>Just as CHRIST loved the church and gave Himself for her</u>'. This is not a conditional love; it is what is expected of any man called Godly. To Love just as CHRIST... How does CHRIST love the Church, He sacrificed for her sins, died for her so she might be redeemed from condemnation and oppression of the evil one.

III. HUSBAND GIVES YOURSELF TO YOUR WIFE...

[25.]*husbands, love your wives, just as CHRIST also loved the church and <u>gave himself for her</u>,'* verse 25

... Sacrificial living for her. Sacrificial life cause woman to submit effortlessly... Selfless and genuine efforts and support to a woman will cause the woman to submit to you effortlessly. Husband is to give himself selflessly, unconditionally to his wife...

IV. HUSBAND TO SANCTIFY, CLEANSE HIS WIFE WITH THE WASHING OF WATER BY THE WORD OF GOD

verse 26. *'That he might sanctify and cleanse her with the washing of water by the word',*

The Godly Man is to be the pastor of his wife: Leading her to the way of GOD. Sanctify comes first before promoting her surrenderness to GOD. Adam missed this first step... Hence raised for himself a woman void of respect for GOD!

In my local church some years ago, a brother, met a lady he likes, encouraged her to attend bible schools, encouraged her to pray more, and encouraged her to love GOD more... Even before proposing to her... What a Godly man! He raised for himself a woman that respect GOD. This is very apt because a woman will multiply in the direction in which she is exposed. Adam was standing by the forbidden tree long enough, not busy tilling the ground or dressing the rest of the garden... giving opportunity for Eve to browse around the Forbidden tree... Hence seeing three reasons why to partake of the tree ('good to look upon', 'would be tasty', 'would give wisdom') versus only one instruction of 'Do not eat of this'.

> *A Godly man shows his wife the way of GOD… raising for himself a woman that respect GOD.*
>
> *This is very apt because a woman will multiply in the direction in which she is exposed.*

Godly investment into any woman will yield great dividend any day and anytime!

This is what the manual says of a Godly Man, expected to be received, believed and acted upon in faith until it becomes a reality in the man.

V. HUSBAND TO NURTURE HIS WIFE UNTIL SHE IS WITHOUT BLEMISH OR SPOT...

Verse 27. *'that he might present her to himself a glorious church, not having spot or wrinkle or any such thing, but that she should be Holy and without blemish.'*

The first ministry of every man is his woman. That means man is responsible for the good behaviour or waywardness of his woman. The way a woman is wired... She multiples whatever she is exposed to. Hence, when you expose or fail to expose your woman to a Godly way... She reproduces the same!

VI. HUSBAND TO LOVE HIS WIFE AS HIS OWN BODY...

Verses 28-29: *'So husbands ought to love their own wives as their own bodies; he who loves his wife loves himself. For no one ever hated his own flesh, but nourishes and cherishes it, just as the Lord does the church.'*

This is giving your woman physical attention. The physical nurture and cherishes of your woman. The woman is already endowed with beauty... Bringing this beauty out is the duty of the Godly man! Making available for her, beauty preparations...clothing, Jewels, shelter, food, comfort, fitness, style. Making her a queen in your palace. No man can do this and miss a supportive, submissive and loving wife... 'People say 'women love money'... maybe it is because women see many things that need to be done and put in place ... a provision gap that needs to be filled by Godly men… Give her beauty preparations… and she will give you smiles all day long!

VII. HUSBAND TO LEAVE HIS FATHER AND MOTHER… AND CLEAVE TO HIS WIFE…

Verse 31: *"'for this reason <u>a man shall leave his father and mother and be joined to his wife</u>, and the two shall become one flesh."*

> *The man has to establish his family. Separating and setting boundaries for extended families…*
>
> *This is the responsibility of the Godly man, not that of his wife!*

And the two shall become one flesh…

The man has to establish his family. Separating and setting boundaries for extended families… While honouring and respecting the extended family is good and expected, the Godly man must place his family first!

Any home that this LEAVING, CLEAVING and BECOMING ONE' is not set in place, there will always be undue interference from the extended families, which will cause undue strains and in many cases serious damage to the home.

This is the responsibility of the Godly man, not that of his wife!. Once this order is set, it becomes easy for the wife to maintain and enjoy a balanced and healthy relationship with her mother-in-law, husband families and her own families as well.

133

My dear friend kindly takes a second look at the above seven qualities of a Godly man… How many of these are you in possession of.

Many have been harassed hence entered marriage with various degrees of wholeness or brokenness… Nevertheless, starting from today, see yourself for real and begin to work on your areas of deficits, engaging the help of the 3rd Person in Marriage, and you will see a Glorious Turnarounds in your home.

The man should focus on his roles to the wife…LOVE, fix you…

The one that instituted marriage has a manual for its effective running… Not applying the manual is to expect undesirable outcomes!

Allow GOD to fix your wife's submission… If men can do these roles, women will easily submit to them!

The one that instituted marriage has a manual for its effective running… Not applying the manual is to expect undesirable outcomes!

Where are you in this radar… Dear Godly man? Which and which of these qualities do you possess right now? Which ones do you need to work on?

Point to note: These duties are not natural…a mere human or carnal man can never manifest them… It takes the alignment with the 3rd person to exhibit them…Because they are the very nature of CHRIST. Yet, GOD is counting on you. He packages the woman for you as a help...However, you need to nurture your help so she might function well for you... The Bible says If your ax is dull... It makes for more strength! When you do your part of the deal... loving and nurturing her in the way of GOD... she brings in all her smartness and intuition to support you, and her beauty to comfort you...

"If the ax is dull, and one does not sharpen the edge, then he must use more strength; but wisdom brings success." (Ecclesiastes 10:10 NKJV).

How helpful is your helpmeet? She was not a ready-made... How much have you invested in her? Spiritually, mentally, socially, morally, financially and physically? How helpful is your helpmeet? Dear Godly Brother? If your ax is dull... Then... Go and sharpen it! Using the manual given...

> ***How helpful is your helpmeet? She was not a ready-made... How much have you invested in her? Spiritually, mentally, socially, morally, financially and physically... Dear Godly Brother...***

There is an understanding that comes with dwelling with woman... Get this understanding, invest in your helpmeet and she will yield greatly for you.

'Husbands, likewise, dwell with them with understanding, giving honor to the wife, as to the weaker vessel, and as being heirs

135

together of the grace of life, that your prayers may not be hindered." (1 peter 3:7, NKJV)

What will you rather do… with this information… He that has an ear… Let him hear what the Spirit says to the churches!

Be that man…with dominion, with authority, with vision, with direction, with stability… Your generation will thank you for this! Remember there is no vacuum in life…When you fail in your duty as a man…Nature tries to adapt…Making the weaker vessel (woman), undertakes what they are not created for… hence the reason for many crises at home, in the community and the world at large.

Where are the Godly men… Where are the Fathers… Where are the nation-builders…

Be one today… Promote one today… Raise one today!

Our GOD is good and His mercies endure forevermore, Amen

Your Notes . . .

How many of the qualities of the Godly man do you possess... How can you improve on them...

The 3rd Person in Marriage

RAISING A GODLY WOMAN

8. RAISING A GODLY WOMAN···

RAISING A GODLY WOMAN...

Let us recall the foundational truth on marriage again...

Adam was created as a male and female... Complete ... Eve is the completing part of Adam... Hence, man and woman are different... and GOD is the 3rd person in marriage ... He joins the man and woman in marriage...

Let us also reminds ourselves of the basic characteristics of the woman in marriage: - Smartness, Intuition and Instincts... Influence... and Beauty to behold.

Woman today is called by so many different names, due to the degrees of wholeness and brokenness she is faced up with and against... So many confusions around womanhood that one wonders why the creation of the woman...

let us look at them now...

THE DIFFERENT NAMES OF WOMAN…

I. GOD CALLS HER . . . THE HELPMEET, A SOLUTION HUB.

"And the Lord GOD said, it is not good that the man should be alone; I will make him <u>an help meet</u> for him." (Genesis 2:18 KJV)

"Now the Lord GOD said, "it is not good (beneficial) for the man to be alone; I will make him a <u>helper [one who balances him--a counterpart who is] suitable and complementary for him</u>." (Genesis 2:18 AMP)

II. ADAM CALLED HER… WOMAN… MY OWN.

[22]"And the rib, which the Lord God had taken from man, made he a woman, and brought her unto the man. [23]<u>And Adam said, this is now bone of my bones, and flesh of my flesh: she shall be called woman</u>, because she was taken out of man. [24]Therefore shall a man leave his father and his mother, and shall cleave unto his wife: and they shall be one flesh. [25]And they were both naked, the man and his wife, and were not ashamed." (Genesis 2:22-25, KJV)

III. SATAN CALLED HER… JEZEBEL … BE ANTI- GOD!

"and it came to pass, as though it had been a trivial thing for him to walk in the sins of Jeroboam the son of Nebat, that he took as wife Jezebel the daughter of Ethbaal, king of the Sidonians; and he went and served Baal and worshipped him." (1 Kings 16:31, NKJV)

"But there was no one like Ahab who sold himself to do wickedness in the sight of the Lord, because Jezebel his wife stirred him up." (1 Kings 21:25, NKJV)

Anti-Godliness ...Influential unto idolatry, Sexual immorality, Witchcrafty...

"Nevertheless I have a few things against you, because you allow that woman Jezebel, who calls herself a prophetess, to teach and seduce my servants to commit sexual immorality and eat things sacrificed to idols." (Revelation 2:20, NKJV)

IV. IN REDEMPTION... SHE IS CALLED THE VIRTUOUS WOMAN.

[10]"Who can find a virtuous wife? For her worth is far above rubies. [11]The heart of her husband safely trusts her; so he will have no lack of gain. [12]She does him good and not evil all the days of her life." (Proverbs 31:10-12, NKJV)

[28]"her children rise up and call her blessed; her husband also, and he praises her: [30]Charm is deceitful and beauty is passing, but a woman who fears the Lord, she shall be praised." (Proverbs 31:28, 30, NKJV)

"Likewise, ye wives, be in subjection to your own husbands; that, if any obey not the word, they also may without the word be won by the conversation of the wives; [2]While they behold your chaste conversation coupled with fear. [3]Whose adorning let it not be that outward adorning of plaiting the hair, and of wearing of gold, or of putting on of apparel; [4]But let it be the hidden man of the heart,

in that which is not corruptible, even the ornament of a meek and quiet spirit, which is in the sight of God of great price. [5]For after this manner in the old time the Holy women also, who trusted in God, adorned themselves, being in subjection unto their own husbands: [6]Even as Sara obeyed Abraham, calling him lord: whose daughters ye are, as long as ye do well, and are not afraid with any amazement." (1 Peter 3:1-6, KJV)

V. IN THE WORLD... SHE IS CALLED ...

Dog, whore, Tools for advertising; Sex tools; Baby mama... Business partner with benefits; friend with benefits; housemate with benefits; a neighbour with benefits; 'holidate' with benefits...

Who are you, dear sister? What is your Name: A helpmeet; Jezebel; A virtuous woman; a sex tool; friend with benefits; baby mama...? Who are you, dear sister! What is your name?

WHY A GODLY WOMAN...

There are too many confusions out there about womanhood. Too many names woman is being called. If left naturally, unguided and unaided... women will operate from the offence side and exhibit all the offence names listed above and some more... Only in redemption can the best of womanhood be seen...

As with raising a Godly man, no mere natural woman can fulfil her roles as a Godly woman. It takes the empowerment of the Holy Ghost to birth a Godly woman.

How then can a Godly woman be raised?

143

THE QUALITIES OF A GODLY WOMAN...

Let us see the manual of marriage again according to the rendition in Ephesians 5:22-33. Everyone is fully captured and covered in this manual.

22"wives, submit to your own husbands, as to the Lord.

23-24For the husband is head of the wife, as also CHRIST is head of the church; And he is the savior of the body. Therefore, just as the church is subject to CHRIST, so let the wives be to their own husbands in everything.

25husbands, love your wives, just as CHRIST also loved the church and gave himself for her,

26-27That he might sanctify and cleanse her with the washing of water by the word, that he might present her to himself a glorious church, not having spot or wrinkle or any such thing, but that she should be Holy and without blemish.

28-29So husbands ought to love their own wives as their own bodies; he who loves his wife loves himself. For no one ever hated his own flesh, but nourishes and cherishes it, just as the Lord does the church.

30For we are members of his body, of his flesh and of his bones.

31"for this reason a man shall leave his father and mother and be joined to his wife, and the two shall become one flesh."

32This is a great mystery, but I speak concerning CHRIST and the church.

[33]Nevertheless let each one of you in particular so love his own wife as himself, and let the wife see that she respects her husband." (Ephesians 5:22-33 NKJV)

Below are the key qualities of a Godly woman:

I SUBMISSION... AS UNTO THE LORD...

"wives, submit to your own husbands, as to the Lord'. (Verse 22)

Submitting unto the husband as you would submit to the Lord. How do we submit to the Lord...

Romans 8:14... Says being led by the Spirit... *'For as many as are led by the Spirit of God, they are the sons of God.' (KJV)*. Choosing to be led by the Spirit, following the inner witness always when making decisions. Making decisions based on what the word of GOD says on the issue and circumstances, not just based on facts and physical presentations.

> **Engaging Silence is a deliberate choice to let the other take a lead. Choosing to go the way of GOD!**

Another very important way to submit to the Lord is through engaging Silence... Silence... Silence... Engaging silence does not connote weakness or being dumb. Engaging Silence is a deliberate choice to let the other take a lead. Choosing to go the way of GOD!

[11]"Let a woman learn in silence with all submission. [12]And I do not permit a woman to teach or to have authority over a man, but to be in silence.

14And Adam was not deceived, but the woman being deceived, fell into transgression. 15Nevertheless she will be saved in childbearing if they continue in faith, love, and holiness, with self-control." (1 Timothy 2:11-12, 14-15, NKJV)

4"But let it be the hidden man of the heart, in that which is not corruptible, even the ornament of a meek and quiet spirit, which is in the sight of God of great price. 5For after this manner in the old time the Holy women also, who trusted in God, adorned themselves, being in subjection unto their own husbands:" (1 Peter 3:4-5 KJV).

How is GOD expecting women to submit to Him... by trusting in the Lord... in prayers...

You submit as a 'PRAY - ER'

How is GOD expecting women to submit to Him... by trusting in the Lord... in prayers... You submit as a pray...er!

One day I asked the Spirit of GOD about the 'Woman in Silence' in the scriptures... with all the characteristics you endowed women with... how can she be in silence with all her smartness, intuition, influence and beauty... Then it was revealed to me... through PRAYING... By channelling all her insights, smartness, intuition and wisdom into prayers....

Remember the talkativeness of the woman... That is a good tool in prayers... When women pray, they do not miss out the details, and GOD loves to hear their voice too...

Woman to be in silence… Help meet in silence… How? Through praying…A woman that does not submit unto the Lord…Cannot submit to her husband… The beginning of submission is the submission in prayers unto GOD.

II. ALLOWING THE MAN TO LEAD…

'For the husband is head of the wife, as also CHRIST is head of the church;' (Verse 23)

In the team…called marriage, Man is the lead…This is a settled matter…Let him be… Remember, a leader does not necessarily know everything …You are to back him up for the success of his leadership …This requires a conscious effort… It is a decision… That must be made…

Allowing your husband to LEAD your home will be a matter of CHOICE… IT IS A DECISION you have to make as a Godly woman.

> *Allowing your husband to LEAD your home will be a matter of CHOICE…*
>
> *IT IS A DECISION you have to make as a Godly woman.*

It is unconditional; it is what the manual says. When the order is set. You can back him up for successful leadership. Not hijacking the leadership from him!

With the Smartness and Intuition of Woman, many easily influenced their husband and

147

hijack the leadership of the family from them. This is not what the manual says...

Allowing your husband to lead will be a matter of CHOICE! It will not often come naturally, the woman has to decide to allow and let the husband lead the family... Period!

III. SUBMISSION IN SUBJECTION IN EVERYTHING...

'Therefore, just as the church is subject to CHRIST, <u>so let the wives be to their own husbands in everything'</u>. (Verse 24)

Spiritually aligning with the spiritual disposition of the husband; Mentally availing him all your smartness and insights and intuition; Making a decision to take a stand on this truth of submitting to your husband is a decision that must be taken consciously and by Choice. It has nothing to do with who your husband it... Is he your husband... then, he is the head of the family.

You choose to submit to him by emotionally aligning with his temperament, physically pleasing him with your beauty and pleasure. Submitting your smartness... Your influence ... and your beauty ... To your man.

This is a decision to be made...When this decision is made... Grace backs you up...

[3]"the older women likewise, that they be reverent in behavior, not slanderers, not given to much wine, teachers of good things— [4]that they admonish the young women to love their husbands, to

love their children, [5]to be discreet, chaste, homemakers, good, obedient to their own husbands, that the word of God may not be blasphemed." (Titus 2:3-5, NKJV)

IV. TOTAL CLEAVING TO THE MAN…

'For this reason, a man shall leave his father and mother <u>and be joined to his wife, and the two shall become one flesh.</u>" (verse 31)

Team up with him…Prioritize him above any other… Especially in public. Being your spouse's No. 1. Fan! It is the quality of a Godly woman! Make it clear that you and your husband decisions are united… Aligning with him as one indeed, especially in the public.

Maintaining the orders and boundaries set by your husband… concerning extended families… Giving respect and honour to whom it is due, however, not overindulging that can harm the cleaving…

V. WOMAN TO RESPECT THE MAN...

'. . . And let the wife see that she respects her husband." (verse 33b).

What is respect… *English dictionary defines respect as: 'A feeling of deep admiration and honour to someone or something elicited from their abilities, qualities and achievements'.* Respect has a lot to do with … Digging out your man's abilities; identifying his achievements and praising him for them; this can be expressed in

149

how you address your man; Always putting forward a touch of honour and appreciation.

To respect someone, there must be tangible attributes of admiration in such a one. Hence, to allow respect flow naturally, it is imperative that the Godly woman deliberate go in search of great attributes of her husband, search for them, seek them, and write them out... why do you like him... Why do you love him? What stands him out among others? Why you said yes to him... all of these could help to promote your respect for him.

Let us take a look at the Amplified Bible rendition of this verse 33b:

'... and the wife [must see to it] that she respects and delights in her husband [that she notices him, and prefers him and treats him with loving concern, treasuring him, honouring him and holding him dear]' (Ephesians 5:33b, AMP)

TAKE A SECOND LOOK AT THIS...

The manual says this is a duty of a Godly woman. No woman attempts the above and the man will not fall headlong in love over her... The manual is clear, however, lack of following the instructions in the manual is what is causing the crisis we see in the world today.

> **When you genuinely identify your man's efforts and achievements and praise him for it... he becomes ecstatic.**

In Mark 4:25... The Bible says that *'To him that has... More shall be given to him. And to him, that has not, Even what he has shall be taken away from him'. (NKJV)*

When you genuinely identify your man's efforts and achievements and praise him for it... he becomes ecstatic.

Especially when the praises are coming from a woman, especially his wife... why, because, having seen much of the woman's smartness and intuition, and have come to respect her judgement, more so, because man always wants to impress his woman... if she can approve and sing praises of him, he feels on top of the whole world!

Man is wired to produce more of such... Praise works well with men...Just like GOD, as we are all made in the image and likeness of GOD. Always have a token of praise... Genuine flattering of praise for your man...And he will be all over you ... It is the manual prescription! Are you a Godly woman...

.

Your Notes . . .

What is the name you are been called, as a woman… or what are you calling your spouse, as a man… what is her name…

Your Notes . . .

What are the qualities of a Godly woman you are possessing right now... How can you improve on this...

The 3rd
Person in
Marriage

THE 3 BASIC

LAWS OF

MARRIAGE

9. THE 3 BASIC LAWS OF MARRIAGE ...

THE MARRIAGE LAWS... LOVE, SUBMISSION AND SEXUAL PURITY...

*T*here are some basic laws that govern Godly Marriage. They are Love, Submission and Sexual Purity. There may be more, however, these three stands out in the scriptures.

I. LOVE...

[6]Dr Roy Harthern, in one of his messages while interviewing and counselling his son in law, Br. Benny Hinn on marriage... (assessed as a public domain video on youtube) said: *'Love is a sacrificial choice that sees the highest and the best for the one who is the object of love... Simply put... Love is putting the other first'...*

---

[6] Dr Roy Harthen was a renowned Bible teacher, Orlando, USA

4"Love suffers long and is kind; love does not envy; love does not parade itself, is not puffed up; 5does not behave rudely, does not seek its own, is not provoked, thinks no evil; 6does not rejoice in iniquity, but rejoices in the truth; 7bears all things, believes all things, hopes all things, endures all things.

8Love never fails. But whether there are prophecies, they will fail; whether there are tongues, they will cease; whether there is knowledge, it will vanish away." (1 Corinthians 13:4-8, NKJV)

This LOVE has two dimensions... Love towards GOD... which will birth the second one... Love towards other men...Genuine love cannot be given without an encounter with the love of GOD...

> **'Love is a sacrificial choice that sees the highest and the best for the one who is the object of love... Simply put... Love is putting the other first'**
>
> **…Dr Roy Harthern**

For GOD is love...

"And we have known and believed the love that God hath to us. GOD is love, and he that dwelleth in love dwelleth in GOD, and GOD in him." (1 John 4:16, KJV)

Only with love for GOD can a man be able to love another... The Bible gave the following dimension of love... Eros... Sensual... Filial... Brotherly... Family Agape... and GOD's kind of love. The bible in Ephesians says of the depth, the length, the breadth and the height of love...

14"For this cause I bow my knees unto the Father of our Lord Jesus Christ, 15Of whom the whole family in heaven and earth is named,

16That he would grant you, according to the riches of his glory, to be strengthened with might by his Spirit in the inner man; 17That CHRIST may dwell in your hearts by faith; that ye, being rooted and grounded in love, 18May be able to comprehend with all saints what <u>is the breadth, and length, and depth, and height</u>; 19And to know the love of CHRIST, which passeth knowledge, that ye might be filled with all the fulness of GOD." (Ephesians 3:14-19, NKJV)

Love is multi-dimensional... *'Love has breath, length, depth and height'.* This makes Love an easy and natural abode for women. If a woman does not love the man because he is wealthy, she will because he can sing, or because he looks good, or because ... of something down the line...

The makeup of the woman makes it easy for her to love...Because of her multi-wired dimension... Smartness...The woman can easily touch on a different level of love... and can eventually get a reason to love the man.

Man on the other side, being unilateral, will always have issue adapting to Love. **This is why Men are more inclined into commitment than the actual love in marriage... and when you do not get a man to commit, you lose his love in a twinkle of an eye!**

Man is not expected to love unilaterally... as the law of love is at all levels... Spiritually, Soulishly... Mentally, in your WIll,

Physically... Man will, therefore, require the empowerment of the Holy Ghost to love.

Ecclesiastes 9:9 says *'Live joyfully with the wife whom thou lovest all the days of the life of thy vanity ...'* The one you love!...

The stability, the unilateral makeup of man... Does not favour love...Hence the emphasis on man to love his wife... For a man to love...He will need GOD. Because love is multilateral... The man struggles with loving someone. Man focuses on one thing at a time: Food; Money; Sex; Business; Family... while giving attention to any of these, others can go to sleep until later!

The stability, the unilateral makeup of man... does not favour love...Hence the emphasis on man to love his wife... For a man to love...He will need GOD.

Woman, on the other hand, link everything together... Her Food is directly related to her Money, to her Sex life, to her Business, to her looks, to her Family... Everything is everything, and all must and should go together... This has caused a lot of confusion... therefore, for a Man to Love, which is multi-lateral, he needs GOD to help link everything together. This is why LOVE YOUR WIFE is a law specifically for Men. Nevertheless, these laws are binding to both the man and the woman...

Your Notes . . .

LOVE is one of the basic law of marriage. How are you loving your spouse... How can you improve on this...

II. SUBMISSION...

This is the ability to yield to a higher authority...GOD always maintain his sovereignty and supremacy from inception... The Bible says that GOD, who puts all in subjection is Himself not put...And He made it clear that all His creatures must reference that... (1 Corinthians 15:27-28).

One of His archangel, Lucifer, ... In Isaiah chapter 14: attempted to break this law... He paid dearly for it...He inherited darkness. He lost his place of abode. And he is condemned for eternal damnation even on the last day... He is Satan and the host of the fallen angels with him. They are the principalities, and demons we have today. He is, therefore, the initiator of rebelliousness.

It is expected that both man and woman be submissive to GOD and themselves. The man's makeup favours submissiveness ... He is unilateral... He is stable... However, the nature of woman repels submission: As a multi-dimensional creature... always questioning everything... Always having many options to choose from... Hence needs to be helped...

> *Submission unto the Lord and to one another is a key law of marriage… Mutual submission becomes easy when submission to GOD is in place.*

Eve saw that the fruit was beautiful to the eyes, will be tasty to the mouth, and also desirous to make one wise... 'Do not eat it' without detailed reasons could not work for her! She had more reasons why she should eat of the forbidden fruit.

Women are prone to rebelling authority...Hence this law of submission is more pronounced for them... 'Be submissive to your husband'. We learnt that when you learn to be submissive unto the Lord, then you can be submissive to your husband.

Nevertheless, Submission unto the Lord and to one another is a key law of marriage... Mutual submission when your submission to GOD is in place.

'Submitting yourselves one to another in the fear of God.' (Ephesians 5:21, KJV).

Your Notes . . .

Submission to the Lord and mutual submission to one another is key in a successful relationship. How are you ensuring this n your marriage...

III. SEXUAL PURITY...

Marriage is honourable in all, and the bed undefiled: but whoremonger and adulterers, God will judge... (Hebrews 13:4 KJV).

The law of sexual purity is not limited to the un-married, It is the law of marriage...Sexual pleasure is only permitted inside the marital covenant... According to the manual in the Kingdom of CHRIST!

> *The singular sin that GOD emphasis as against one own body and soul is sexual immorality...*
>
> *All sexual sins will be judged... before ... during and after marriage...*

'Marriage is honourable in all, and the bed undefiled: but whoremongers and adulterers God will judge.' (Hebrews 13:4, KJV)

Let us see the Amplified Bible rendition of this verse:

'Marriage is to be held in honour among all [that is, regarded as something of great value], and the marriage bed undefiled [by immorality or by any sexual sin]; for God will judge the sexually immoral and adulterous.' (Hebrews 13:4, AMP)

Yes...We are not of this world...Yes... we are to follow this manual, or suffer the undesirable outcomes of breaking this law. The singular sin that GOD emphasis as against one own body and soul

164

is sexual immorality... All sexual sins will be judged... before ... during and after marriage...

"Thou shalt not commit adultery." (Exodus 20:14, KJV)

"But whoso committeth adultery with a woman lacketh understanding: he that doeth it destroyeth his own soul." (Proverbs 6:32 KJV)

===========================

Understanding how GOD valued His temple while He was still residing at The Tabernacles in the days of Moses can throw some lights into how GOD values our Bodies as His Temple now…

===========================

"Whosoever putteth away his wife, and marrieth another, committeth adultery: and whosoever marrieth her that is put away from her husband committeth adultery." (Luke 16:18, KJV)

The only ground ... The scripture permit separation in marriage...

Our body is the temple of the Most High... Hence, must be valued as such. Understanding how GOD valued His temple while He was still residing at The Tabernacles in the days of Moses can throw some lights into how GOD values our Bodies as His Temple now… Not everybody can approach the Tabernacle; even the priests were not permitted to approach without proper and due order, preparations and specific time for worship… This Temple has now become our bodies… GOD ceases to dwell in a physically built temple, now residing inside the Spirit of Christians...

This is why defiling your body as a Christian is simply dishonouring the Temple of GOD and it attracts great penalties.

[15]*"know ye not that your bodies are the members of CHRIST? Shall I then take the members of CHRIST, and make them the members of an harlot? GOD forbid.* [16]*What? Know ye not that he which is joined to an harlot is one body? For two, saith he, shall be one flesh.* [17]*But he that is joined unto the Lord is one Spirit.*

[18]*Flee fornication. Every sin that a man doeth is without the body, but he that committeth fornication sinneth against his own body.* [19]*What? Know ye not that your body is the temple of the Holy Ghost which is in you, which ye have of God, and ye are not your own?* [20]*For ye are bought with a price: therefore glorify God in your body, and in your Spirit, which are GOD's."* (1 Corinthians 6:15-20, KJV)

> **Defiling your body with immoralities as a Christian is simply dishonouring the Temple of GOD and it attracts great penalties**

JESUS CHRIST took it a bit higher... and stricter... Focusing on being accountable even at the thought level...No wonder He did not condemn the woman claimed caught at adultery... Because although He was not approving of her sins, He also was disapproving the fact that she sinned when she was caught... Long before she committed the sins, while in her thoughts, she already sinned and was judged!

166

[4]*"They say unto him, master, this woman was taken in adultery, in the very act.* [5]*Now Moses in the law commanded us, that such should be stoned: but what sayest thou?*

[7]*So when they continued asking him, he lifted up himself, and said unto them, He that is without sin among you, let him first cast a stone at her." (John 8:4-5, 7, KJV)*

Our Lord JESUS CHRIST emphatically showed that sins are measured at the thought level...

[27]*"Ye have heard that it was said by them of old time, thou shalt not commit adultery:*

[28]*But I say unto you, That whosoever looketh on a woman to lust after her hath committed adultery with her already in his heart.* [29]*And if thy right eye offends thee, pluck it out, and cast it from thee: for it is profitable for thee that one of thy members should perish, and not that thy whole body should be cast into hell." (Matthew 5:27-29, KJV)*

Hebrews says our Lord JESUS CHRIST was tempted as we are … Yet without sin... How... because He conquered them at the thought level hence no occasion for their manifestations...

[14]*"seeing then that we have a great high priest, that is passed into the heavens, JESUS the son of GOD, let us hold fast our profession.* [15]*For we have not an high priest which cannot be touched with the feeling of our infirmities; but was in all points tempted like as we are, yet without sin." (Hebrews 4:14-15, KJV).*

167

Sins are measured at the thought level...The physical manifestation is only the outcome of sins...

In our book [7]*__Understanding the works of darkness'__*... we dealt extensively on the topic 'Sin Dynamics', there the different formative stages of sins are revealed and especially how to overcome them in Grace. You may avail yourself of this book, we pray it BLESSES you.

Sins are measured at the thought level...The physical manifestation is only the outcome of sins...

The good news to this is that... **As sins are measured at the thoughts level, so also can you conquer sins at the thought level and you will not get to manifest them physically! Once you overcome it at the thought level... You have defeated sins...**

The Book of James explains this...

[13]*"let no man say when he is tempted, I am tempted of GOD: for GOD cannot be tempted with evil, neither tempteth he any man:* [14]*But every man is tempted, when he is drawn away of his own lust, and enticed.* [15]*Then when lust hath conceived, it bringeth forth sin: and sin, when it is finished, bringeth forth death.* [16]*Do not err, my beloved brethren.* [17]*Every good gift and every perfect gift is from above, and cometh down from the father of lights, with whom is no variableness, neither shadow of turning.* [18]*Of his own*

---

[7] 'Understanding the works of darkness'... available on amazon.com

will begat he us with the word of truth, that we should be a kind of firstfruits of his creatures." (James 1:13-18, KJV)

Engaging the will of a man to choose... Man and woman can engage their will to choose sexual purity. For only what you choose is permitted to happen to you.

¹⁵ *"see, I have set before thee this day life and good, and death and evil;*

¹⁹*I call heaven and earth to record this day against you, that I have set before you life and death, blessing and cursing: therefore choose life, that both thou and thy seed may live:" (Deuteronomy 30:15, 19, KJV)*

One day, the Spirit of GOD gave me this revelation:

The abilities of good are of GOD... The abilities of evil are of Darkness… However, the WILL to make a CHOICE is of Man, When Man makes a CHOICE, the corresponding ABILITIES back him… Now, Man will be responsible for the CHOICES he makes, today and on the day of judgement!.

 Pause, Ponder and think about this!

As a Christian, you can and should rebuke the Spirit of lust and they will bow at the Name of JESUS CHRIST! If you do not take action against the influence of sexual immoralities in your life… they will have a free ride over your life. Stand up against it. Choose sexual purity, rebuke the forces of darkness, do this right at the thought level, long before the opportunity for its manifestations show up… and you will never be a victim of such sins again.

This sexual purity law is for both the man and the woman… However. remember that beauty is one of the characteristics of a woman…Hence, men may need to work extra on this law… because men will always have an eye for the beauty of women!

Simply declaring that 'I CHOOSE SEXUAL PURITY'… and saying this repeatedly especially when THE THOUGHTS FOR IMMORALITIES present themselves… will attract GOD's abilities to back you. **There must be a pre-decision for sexual purity… For you to overcome it…**

STEPPING AWAY FROM HABITUAL SINNING… ENGAGING THE GRACE OF GOD…

SIN is a sure entrance of darkness into anyone's life. 1 John 3:8a says *'He that committeth sin is of the devil;…'* The Good news, however, is … There is GRACE available to overcome all sins and habitual additions…

HOW…

Anytime you go to GOD genuinely in repentance, seeking for MERCY… you are entering the Throne of GRACE… before you leave, GRACE is administered unto you to overcome… If you continue this repeatedly when you fall into sin… very soon, you would have received enough GRACE to overcome the sin or addition! … (Hebrews. 4:16)

'Let us therefore come boldly unto the throne of grace, that we may obtain mercy, and find grace to help in time of need.' (Hebrews 4:16, KJV)

The place is called ... THE THRONE OF GRACE...

What is administer is... GRACE...

The Passcode is... MERCY.

Think about this... (Hebrews 4:16).

These Marriage laws... Love, Submission and Sexual Purity...What will you do with this information ... Breaking them will expose you to the enemy to steal, to kill and to destroy... Keeping these laws will endear you unto GOD... The Spirit of marriage... When you fulfil your part, you are committing GOD to fulfil His! Our GOD is good and His mercies endure forevermore, Amen

Your notes. . .

Sexual Purity... why is this so important today before or during marriage...

Your Notes . . .

How are you overcoming sexual sins in your life...

MANAGING CRISIS OF THE PREPARATIONS IN MARRIAGE

10. MANAGING CRISIS OF THE PREPARATIONS IN MARRIAGE···

MANAGING CRISIS OF THE PREPARATIONS IN MARRIAGE….

*A*lthough, this book had spelt out some detailed expected preparations that may make for a great relationship in marriage, In reality, this is not always the case. We all have different and various backgrounds, cultures, communities and beliefs… varied exposures to what we claimed to be the norms and standards of living. Yet, we are faced with making decisions for marriage. We, therefore, bring our degree of brokenness and wholeness to the relationship, making the relationship doomed from the start!

When I encountered the 3rd Person of Marriage, The Spirit of Marriage, He revealed that if men do not attempt to put asunder, what He joined together would stand… Irrespective of the degree of brokenness and wholeness, when you are in the covenant of marriage with your spouse and GOD, He steps in to make the amends. HE WORKS THE MIRACLE. In other words, every marriage is a MIRACLE! **There is no born successful marriage, every marriage is a miracle. You now have to seek for your Marriage Miracle.**

Common now, with all the baggage you were faced up with from your young, is it possible you make a good man or a good woman... even if you can vouch for yourself, can you say the same about your spouse. The good ones always attract the very 'bad' ones... (I wonder why)

> *Irrespective of the degree of brokenness and wholeness, if you are in the covenant of marriage with your spouse and GOD, GOD steps in to make the amends.*
>
> *GOD WORKS THE MIRACLE...*

Therefore, in this chapter, we will be going through the step by step of how to access your customised MARITAL MIRACLE.

This is a very important aspect of this book... As knowledge without application is not beneficial. In this session, we will be working with you as you attempt with the help of the Holy Ghost to translate the knowledge acquired into a fruitful application for a change of story for the better in your marriage.

With GOD, all things are possible... If you are willing, you can access the customised miracle for your marriage...

177

POINTS OF RECORD …

- This book should be read together as a couple... However, even if you are alone in the journey of seeking your customized miracle...or you are single preparing for your great relationship... It is still okay... The 3rd Person is here to team with you.

- At the end of each chapter, we asked you to write down points you gained and how you wish to apply them; now is the time to apply them...

- This is a weekly plan... deeply looking into your life and that of your spouse (if married), and seeing how much you align with the manual of marriage...

- You will be writing some notes, one for yourself and one for your spouse... and compare notes after (if you are already in a relationship)... Or else, you do it solely for yourself if you are single.

- You may get a mentor or a supporting friend to support you during this exercise... for accountability … All the very best!

- Be sincere as much as possible to get the best from this exercise... Remember, this is a good investment into your life and destiny... GREAT GRACE … in the Name of YESHUA HAMASHIACH (JESUS CHRIST), Amen.

WEEK 1...

UNDERSTANDING MARRIAGE....

Let us take a second quick recap of the Basic Truth we learnt so far...

The Man at creation...Eve is the part of Man. Man and woman are different... and the 3rd Person in Marriage...

How receptive are you to this understanding...

The Man in Marriage... What are the qualities of the Man in Marriage... How many of them do you (or your spouse) possess... What causes the lack...

The Woman in Marriage... What are the qualities of the Woman in Marriage... How many of them do you (or your spouse) possess... What causes a lack of it...

Share notes… Compare notes… Pray together…

Forgive all hurts…

Forgive misunderstandings…

Forgive the wrong background…

Forgive wrong assumptions…

Now… Your spouse needs you… The 3rd Person in Marriage is ready to give you your customised miracles…

How much of the deficits can you tolerate… How much are you willing to change… How ready are you to allow the 3rd Person to fix you both… There is a CUSTOMISED MIRACLE for both of you… Seek for this… Pray for this… and you will experience it…

PRAYERS POINTS …

SPEND SOME TIME TO PRAY TOGETHER ON YOUR DISCOVERIES…

COMMIT YOUR SPOUSE UNTO THE LORD… ALLOWING THE 3RD PERSON TO HELP YOU AND YOUR SPOUSE…

THANK GOD BY FAITH FOR ANSWERS TO PRAYERS…

Write out your NEW and customised Understanding of Marriage… based on your situations and circumstances … letting GOD free hand to fix you both…

WEEK 2 …

IDENTIFYING WHERE YOU ARE AT THE PREPARATION RADAR OF MARRIAGE…

In this session, we will be looking into the very root cause of our personalities … We will be searching deep into what and what informed your present dispositions to marriage… And if you are still single, (all the better)... You will have the opportunity to see the possible flaws and what and what to amend before entering that beautiful union. If you are already married, (still in order)… you will be able to see why things are working, or why they are not working, and what can be done about them…

It is advisable to do this together as a couple, and compare notes, however, if you are alone on this journey, it is still good. You have the 3rd Person in Marriage to team with…

Remember, you will be writing out for yourself as well as for your spouse…. However, you are allowed to do for yourself if you are still single and not in a relationship yet…

Let us do this… Praying that as you take a dive into the foundation of your life and that of your spouse, GOD will grant you insights and revelations of what to encourage, what to fix, and what to accept and tolerate… in the Name of YESHUA HAMASHIACH, (JESUS CHRIST), Amen.

RAISING THE BOY FOR MARRIAGE...

How were you (or your spouse) raised as a boy child... Ask questions and write them down...

What was your father or father figure (of your spouse) attributes like...

What was your mother or mother figure (of your spouse) attributes like...

The SEED OF MANHOOD… Authority and Dominion; Vision and Direction… and Stability… Do you (or your spouse) possess these qualities…

If you (or your spouse) lack any or all of them, what was responsible for the lack …

How can you build this up…

How can you help your spouse build these qualities up…

(Check the chapter on Preparing a boy for Marriage for details)…

RAISING THE GIRL FOR MARRIAGE...

How were you (or your spouse) raised as a girl child... Ask questions and write them down...

What was your father or father figure's (of your spouse) attributes like...

What was your mother or mother figure's (of your spouse) attributes like...

The HELP MEET ... Smartness and Intuition... Influence... Beauty...
Do you (or your spouse) possess these qualities...

If you (or your spouse) lack any or all of them, what was responsible for the lack …

How can you build this up…

How can you help your spouse build these qualities up…

(Check the chapter on Preparing a girl for Marriage for details)…

Share notes… Compare notes… Pray together…

Forgive all hurts…

Forgive misunderstandings…

Forgive the wrong background…

Forgive wrong assumptions…

Now… Your spouse needs you… The 3rd Person in Marriage is ready to give you your customised miracles…

How much of the deficits can you tolerate… How much are you willing to change… How ready are you to allow the 3rd Person to fix you both…

There is a CUSTOMISED MIRACLE for both of you… Seek for this… Pray for this… and you will experience it…

PRAYERS POINTS …

SPEND SOME TIME TO PRAY TOGETHER ON YOUR DISCOVERIES…

COMMIT YOUR SPOUSE UNTO THE LORD… ALLOWING THE 3RD PERSON TO HELP YOU AND YOUR SPOUSE…

THANK GOD BY FAITH FOR ANSWERS TO PRAYERS…

Write out your NEW and customised Marriage VALUES... based on your situations and circumstances ... letting GOD free hand to fix you both...

Congratulations...

WEEK 3 . . .

CHECKING OUT YOUR QUALITIES AS A GODLY MAN...

(Both of you are to do this... and compare notes afterwards)...

What are the qualities of a Godly Man...

How many of these qualities do you (or your spouse) possess... Ask questions... and write them down...

Are you (or your spouse) the head of your family...

If not... what happened... what is stopping you ... Ask question...

Do you as a man (or your spouse) LOVE your wife sacrificially and unconditionally... If not, what is stopping you ...

Do you as a man (or your spouse) GIVE to your wife willingly and sacrificially... If not... what is stopping you ...

Do you as a man (or your spouse) teach your wife in the ways of the Lord... If not... what is stopping you ...

Do you as a man (or your spouse) nurture, protect and guide your wife /fiancée until she is without blemish or spot... helping her with her weaknesses and flaws...

Do you as a man (or your spouse) love your wife as your own body... caring physically for her... If not... what is stopping you...

Do you as a man (or your spouse) initiates leaving your father and mother and cleave to your wife… Setting boundary for your family…

If not… what is stopping you …

If you or your spouse lack any or all of them, what is responsible for the lack …

How can you build this up…

How can you help your spouse build these qualities up…

 (Check the chapter on Raising a Godly Man for Marriage for details)…

Write out at least 10 things you love about your woman...

CHECKING OUT YOUR QUALITIES AS A GODLY WOMAN...

(Both of you are to do this... and compare notes afterwards)...

What are the qualities of a Godly Woman...

How many of these qualities do you (or your spouse) possess... Ask questions... and write them down...

Are you as a woman (or your spouse) submissive to your husband as unto the Lord... A sincere submission...

If not... what happened... what is stopping you ... Ask questions...

Do you as a woman (or your spouse) allowing your husband to be the leader of your family... If not, what is stopping you ...

Are you as a woman (or your spouse) submissive in everything, or just in few things… If not, what is stopping you …

Do you as a woman (or your spouse) align with your man's boundaries by cleaving to him, being his No.1. Fan especially in Public … If not… what is stopping you …

Do you as a woman (or your spouse) respect your man… This is identifying what you like about him and praise him for them…

Write out at least 10 things you like and respect about your man...

If you or your spouse lack any or all of them, what was responsible for the lack …

How can you build this up…

How can you help your spouse build these qualities up…

Share notes... Compare notes... Pray together...

Forgive all hurts...

Forgive misunderstandings...

Forgive the wrong background...

Forgive wrong assumptions...

Now... Your spouse needs you... The 3rd Person in Marriage is ready to give you your customised miracles...

How much of the deficits can you tolerate... How much are you willing to change... How ready are you to allow the 3rd Person to fix you both...

There is a CUSTOMISED MIRACLE for both of you... Seek for this... Pray for this... and you will experience it...

PRAYERS POINTS ...

SPEND SOME TIME TO PRAY TOGETHER ON YOUR DISCOVERIES...

COMMIT YOUR SPOUSE UNTO THE LORD... ALLOWING THE 3RD PERSON TO HELP YOU AND YOUR SPOUSE...

THANK GOD BY FAITH FOR ANSWERS TO PRAYERS...

Write out your NEW and customised EXPECTED QUALITIES for your Marriage … based on your situations and circumstances … allowing GOD free hand to fix you both…

Congratulations…

CHECKING OUT YOUR ADHERENCE TO THE LAWS OF MARRIAGE…

(Both of you are to do this… and compare notes afterwards)…

There are three basic Laws of Marriage…. Love, Submission and Sexual Purity…

LOVE…

Write out 5 things you love about your spouse…

Write out 5 ways you want your spouse to express Love to you...

Write out 5 things you are struggling on about how to express your Love to your spouse…

(Be plain to your spouse… and The 3rd Person will heal you both… in the Name of YESHUA HAMASHIACH (JESUS CHRIST), Amen.

SUBMISSION...

Write out 5 ways you show RESPECT and SUBMISSION to GOD...

Write out 5 things you RESPECT about your spouse...

Write out 5 ways you want your spouse to RESPECT you…

Write out 5 things you are struggling about on how to RESPECT your spouse...

What are the 5 key ways you show SUBMISSION to your spouse...

SEXUAL PURITY ...

Write out 5 ways you are upholding sexual purity...

Write out 5 ways you are struggling about sexual purity...

Hmmmmmm....

Share notes... Compare notes... Pray together...

Forgive all hurts...

Forgive misunderstandings...

Forgive the wrong background...

Forgive wrong assumptions...

Now... Your spouse needs you... The 3rd Person in Marriage is ready to give you your customised miracles...

How much of the deficits can you tolerate... How much are you willing to change... How ready are you to allow the 3rd Person to fix you both...

There is a CUSTOMISED MIRACLE for both of you... Seek for this... Pray for this... and you will experience it...

PRAYERS POINTS ...

SPEND SOME TIME TO PRAY TOGETHER ON YOUR DISCOVERIES...

COMMIT YOUR SPOUSE UNTO THE LORD... ALLOWING THE 3RD PERSON TO HELP YOU AND YOUR SPOUSE...

THANK GOD BY FAITH FOR ANSWERS TO PRAYERS...

Write out your NEW and customised MARITAL LAWS for your union ... based on your situations and circumstances ... allowing GOD free hand to fix you both...

Congratulations...

If you follow these steps faithfully... Just attempting it will endear you to your spouse if you are already in a relationship... It would have shed lights on some of the grey areas of your life and what you can improve upon while waiting for your Mr Right or Miss Right...

Like we said earlier... Marriage is a Miracle. There is a customized Miracle for your relationship based on your peculiarities... Deciding to allow the 3rd Person step in and take His rightful place is the main key to a Blissful Relationship.

And, if you seem alone in the journey of creating your customized miracle... Just doing your part of the deal by aligning with the 3rd Person in Marriage... The two of you... (GOD and You) are two agreeing together... and it is enough to sort things out.

This is just the Preparatory Stage of Marriage... Focusing on what went wrong or what is right about the foundation of your marriage. If this is diligently sorted out... as a good foundation, every other thing will fit in well.

My dear friend, what will you rather do with this information... Will you like to share it with a friend that may appreciate it. Remember to keep your copy discreet. Let your friends get their copies...

. . . there are still more.

THE 3RD PERSON IN MARRIAGE SERIES . . .

When the Spirit of GOD nudged me to take on this series, I was super reluctant... who will not, for this was where I failed the most in my life - Marriage... (I thought!)... However, right in the deepest valley of my failure.... I encountered the 3rd Person in Marriage, who began to reveal to me, step by step, precept upon precept, line upon line... how and why marriages fail... and why Marriage can be successful!

Like everything created and valued by GOD, the enemy attacks Marriage immensely at every stage of its life cycle... – The understanding stage, (wrong perspective and beliefs on marriage); preparatory stage, (wrong upbringing and abused childhood); choosing stage, (wrong timing and choice of partners, or lack of partner); fusion stage, (incompatibility at different levels); multiplication stage, (unfruitfulness physically, socially and spiritually); and reigning stage, (living in fulfilment in life)...

This book series will show you WHY your marriage is working, so you might keep at it ... or WHY it is not working, so you might see a customized way out for you...

Now that we have journeyed through the Preparations for Marriage... It is time to look into the other aspects of the marriage cycle. We pray they BLESS you too...

CHOOSING IN MARRIAGE...

Choosing in Marriage... After a seasoned foundation... The choice you make is very crucial. This book focuses on why you need to discover you before choosing; Are there boundaries in choosing; When to and when not to choose; How to engage divine Helpers; Finally, and she said yes! ... and managing crisis of choosing and singleness in marriage...

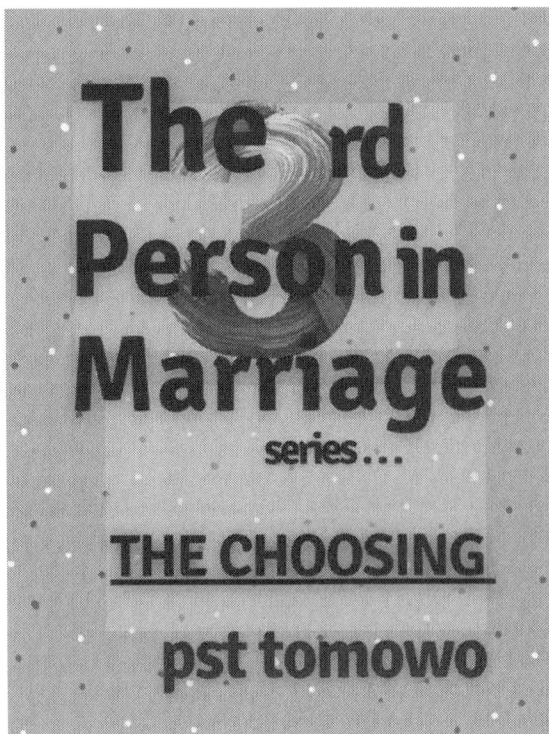

THE COMPATIBILITIES … IN MARRIAGE…

The Compatibilities in Marriage… There are different levels of compatibilities, with varied requirements… Many today tolerate their unions and live in hell daily because of incompatibilities lacuna… This book focuses on compatibilities at different levels such as Physical, Mental, Spiritual, and Social compatibilities; Dealing with gifted spouse… and managing the crisis of compatibility In marriage. And how to avoid them…

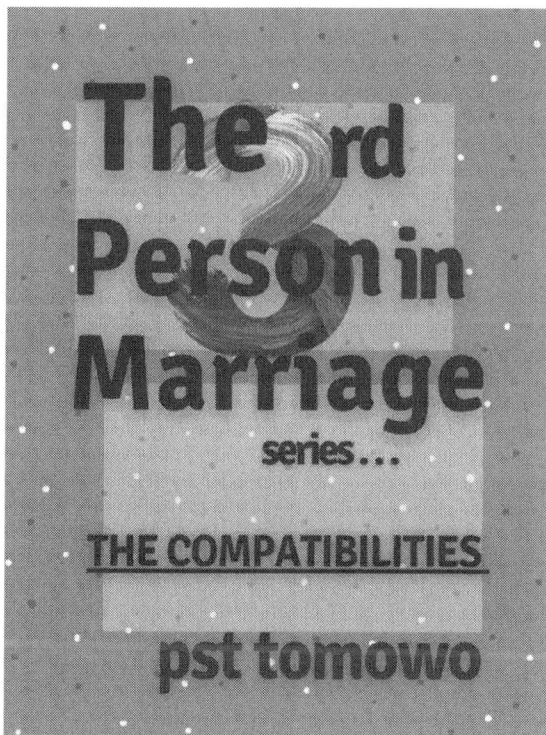

The 3rd Person in Marriage series …

THE COMPATIBILITIES

pst tomowo

MULTIPLICATIONS... IN MARRIAGE...

The multiplications in Marriage... Not only is Marriage to be enjoyed, it is also expected to be fruitful... Can Marriage birth multiplications? Why is mine not? This focuses on Physical fruitfulness; Spiritual fruitfulness, Financial fruitfulness, Social fruitfulness, and managing crisis of multiplications in marriage.

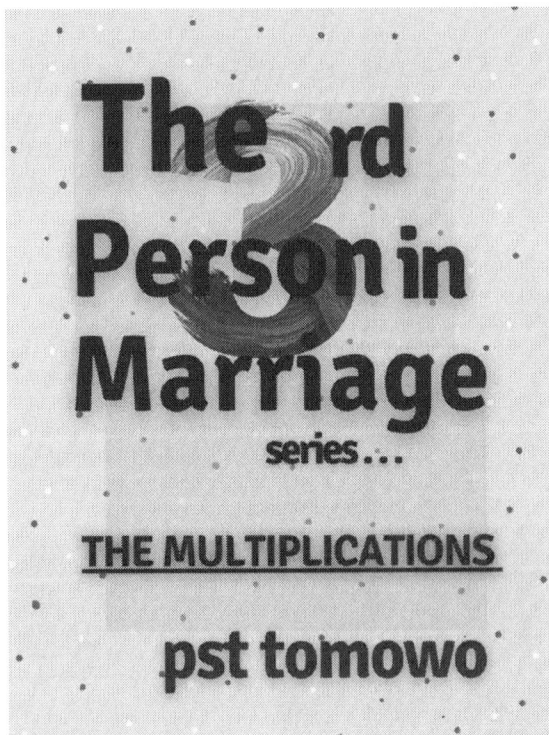

REIGNING... IN MARRIAGE...

The Reigning in Marriage... The original purpose of GOD creating man is to be fruitful, multiply, fill the earth, subdue and have dominion. This is expected to be reflected in marriage... This book Focuses on Enforcing Dominion in marriage; Invoking Generational BLESSING; Establishing the light that shines; Giving helping Hands to younger couples... and managing the crisis of reigning in marriage... among others.

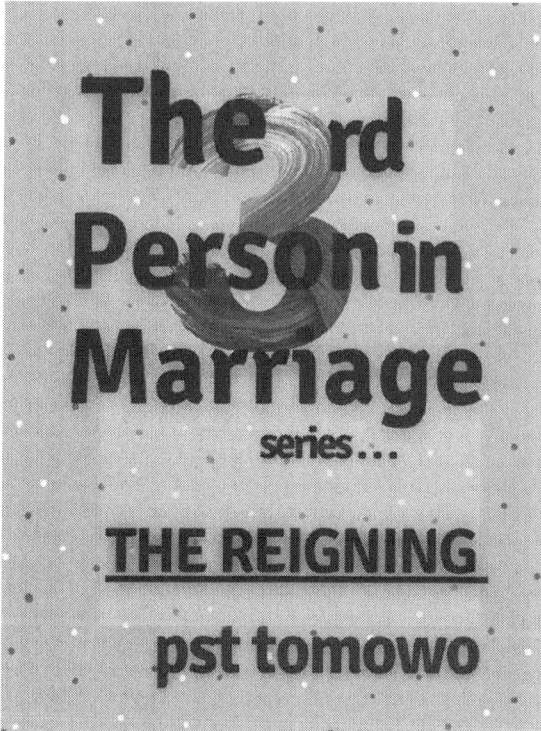

The 3rd Person in Marriage series...

THE REIGNING

pst tomowo

PRAYER OF SALVATION ···

Lord Jesus, I believe you are the SON of GOD that came to the world, died on the cross for all Sins, Iniquities, and Transgressions, by your BLOOD redeemed man from all sins, and their consequences, from all curses, and delivered man from the authority of darkness, and translated them into your kingdom.

[8]I believe I, therefore, receive and confess you JESUS CHRIST as my Lord and Saviour. Thank you for dying for me and forgiving me my sins. I receive by faith the forgiveness of my sins, the Authority, the Power to become a son of GOD, with the Gift of Righteousness, a Right Standing with GOD and the Deliverance from Satan and all the forces of darkness. I am a new creature now, old things are passed away. Everything becomes new, thank you, Lord, I am born again. Amen. Alleluia.

Lord JESUS, you said you would send the HOLY SPIRIT to us to help us, teach us, comfort us, strengthen and reveal all truth to us. Now that I am born again, I ask by faith for the Baptism of the HOLY GHOST in JESUS Name, Amen. Thank you because I have received HIM Now, HE is mine; I give you GLORY, Amen. I speak by faith and trust that the HOLY SPIRIT will give me UTTERANCE now in JESUS NAME, AMEN.

THANK YOU . . .

Thank you for reading this piece. We pray that it BLESSES you as it is BLESSING us too...

My dear friend, what will you rather do with this information?

Please share your experiences with us, email us at info@air.church and let us celebrate with you on how this book has in any way helped in creating your customised marriage miracle. Thank you for the opportunity to share with you.

Expecting your testimonies. . .

Our GOD is GOOD and HIS MERCIES endure forevermore, Amen.

... pst tomowo
... setting men up with GOD, for a Glorious Turnaround.

some more ...

JESUS CHRIST... my Substitute, my Sacrifice, my Inheritance...

it starts with a substitution, followed by the sacrifice, then the inheritance. Until Christians lay hold on this truth, questions and doubts around the realities of CHRIST's existence and purpose for mankind will linger on . . ..

I'm a STAR! . . .
Managing the gifting and the gifted

Gifting can be as little as your name always come up...Many gifted people are bullied, oppressed, suppressed, simply because people around them lack the understanding of WHY and HOW to manage the gift

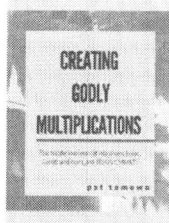

Creating GODLY Multiplications

The hidden secrets of Abraham, Isaac, Jacob and our Lord JESUS CHRIST to GODLY Multiplications. Also revealing how one can apply them in today's world and circumstances.

The LIFE Coaching ...

This is an online coaching platform with pst tomowo, an online retreat where we set men up with GOD for a Glorious Turnaround.

*For more information on these ... Email us: **info@air.church**

Notes . . .

MEET PST TOMOWO ···

'Tomowo Faduyile George (pst tomowo) is a passionate lover of GOD.

A dynamic and prophetic teacher of the WORD with a vivid presence of GOD's Anointing.

A trained pharmacist, expert in public health, a lover of people, team player, peace-loving, gentle and beautiful lady.

pst tomowo is called into teaching and ministering of GOD's GRACE, endowed with GOD's Presence, Power and Goodness.

She is known for her soft touch of motherly love, ready to Give, BLESS and Support. Having been through and overcome several long standing, life challenges, HELPED by GOD, pst tomowo pulls from this depth, always armed with a sweet smile and a word of encouragement for anyone that meets her, every time.

She is easily drawn to people in need, especially women, young adults and children.

She is a Life Coach, an author, artist, dynamic teacher of the Word, runs an all-online Faith based LIFE Coaching, accessible worldwide for retreats, self helps, mentoring and encounters for breakthrough... She also runs other online broadcasts...

Printed by Amazon Italia Logistica S.r.l.
Torrazza Piemonte (TO), Italy

17284302R00142